Appetizers

Hors d'Oeuvres to Light Meals

By the Editors of Sunset Books
and Sunset Magazine

Lane Publishing Co. · Menlo Park, California

Setting the party mood . . .

Good food is a big part of a good party, whether it's a casual evening with a few close friends or a grand afternoon occasion for a multitude. In this book you'll find recipes for the foods you'll love to serve for such widely different occasions—and for all kinds in between.

Snacks to nibble between meals; crisp bite-size enticements; versatile spreads and dips; invitingly hot baked pastries; wonderfully meaty morsels; and marvelous first-course salads, soups, and pastas—they're all here. Choose the lightest for a mere teasing of appetites, or orchestrate a medley of foods that will collectively make an hors d'oeuvre meal.

Relaxation is the prevailing mood of the most memorable parties. When you've heeded the advice on planning your party and its menu, then made use of the do-ahead tips offered in most of our recipes, you'll find yourself in as much of a party mood as any guest!

For their generosity in sharing props for use in our photographs, we'd like to thank Allied Arts Traditional Gift Shop, Best of All Worlds, B.I.A. Cordon Bleu, Brass International, Hammock Way, House of Today, Menlo Park Hardware Co., S. Christian of Copenhagen, William Ober Co., and Williams-Sonoma Kitchenware. And for her thorough and thoughtful editing of the manuscript, we extend special thanks to Fran Feldman.

Research & Text: *Cynthia Scheer*

Coordinating Editor: *Helen Sweetland*

Design: *Lea Damiano Phelps*

Illustrations: *Jacqueline Osborn*

Photography: *Nikolay Zurek* (7, 15, 23, 26, 31, 34, 42, 50, 55, 58, 63, 66, 71, 74, 79, 82, 87, 90, 95)

Darrow M. Watt (2, 10, 18, 39, 47)

Photo Editor: *Lynne B. Morrall*

Cover: Stripes of emerald-green pesto accent a spectacular party appetizer, Layered Cheese Torta with Pesto (page 24). Serve it to spread on sliced French bread and an assortment of crisp raw vegetables. Photograph by Nikolay Zurek. Cover design by Naganuma Design and Lynne B. Morrall.

Sunset Books
  Editor, David E. Clark
  Managing Editor, Elizabeth L. Hogan

Fourth printing July 1988

Spinach-wrapped Chicken gilded with Curry Mayonnaise offers a glimpse of the treats ahead. The recipe is on page 62.

Contents

Light Bites

Irresistible, seasoned nuts to serve by the bowlful, mouth-watering morsels of beef and pea pods to pick up and nibble, and a tempting mélange of marinated fresh vegetables to pop into your mouth—these are the kinds of light bites you'll discover in this chapter.

Our festive, yet easy-to-make appetizers are the welcome kind you can have on hand for the spur-of-the-moment occasion or prepare well ahead for a party. Offer one or two for a casual evening at home with friends or family; for an hors d'oeuvre buffet or a dinner party, arrange half a dozen colorful, elegant-looking appetizers on a handsome tray for a variety of bite-size enticements.

Chili Peanuts

Pictured on page 58

2 cups (about 11 oz.) raw Spanish
  peanuts
2 teaspoons chili powder

1 teaspoon ground cumin
3 small dried whole hot red chiles

1 tablespoon salad oil
  Salt

These spicy nibbles will disappear quickly. Look for raw peanuts in health food stores.

*P*lace peanuts in a 10 by 15-inch rimmed baking pan. Bake in a 350° oven, stirring occasionally, for about 15 minutes or until nuts are pale gold. Remove from oven and add chili powder, cumin, dried chiles, and oil. Mix well. Return to oven and continue baking, stirring once, for 8 to 10 more minutes or until nuts are golden brown. Sprinkle with salt to taste.

Serve warm or cool. To store, place in an airtight container and keep in a cool place for up to a week. Makes 2 cups.

Candied Pecans

Pictured on page 7

¾ cup water
3 tablespoons sugar
2 tablespoons honey

2 cups (about 8 oz.) pecan halves
  Salad oil

The shiny mahogany-hued coating on these pecans comes from simmering them in a honey syrup, then frying them.

*I*n a 2 to 3-quart pan, bring water, sugar, and honey to a boil. Boil, uncovered, for 1 minute. Add nuts and reduce heat to medium; cook, stirring occasionally, until almost all the liquid has evaporated (about 15 minutes).

Meanwhile, pour oil to a depth of 1 to 1½ inches into a wok or 10-inch frying pan. Place over medium heat until oil reaches 275° on a deep-frying thermometer. With a slotted spoon, transfer candied nuts into hot oil. Cook, stirring often and maintaining oil temperature, until nuts turn deep golden brown (7 to 9 minutes)—watch carefully to prevent burning. Quickly lift out nuts so they don't stick together. Let cool on a pan until glaze is hard.

If made ahead, store at once (nuts absorb moisture quickly) in an airtight container in a cool place for up to 2 days. Makes 2 cups.

Crisp-fried Onions

2 large onions (about 1 lb. *total*)
½ cup all-purpose flour

  Salad oil
  Salt

These warm, crisply fried onions are marvelous with wine or an apéritif.

*P*eel and thinly slice onions; then separate into rings. Place flour in a bag, add onions, and shake to coat evenly with flour.

In a deep 2½ to 3-quart pan over high heat, bring 1½ inches oil to 300° on a deep-frying thermometer. Add onions, about a fourth at a time, and cook, stirring often, until golden (about 5 minutes). Oil temperature will drop at first, then rise as onions brown; regulate heat accordingly.

With a slotted spoon, lift out onions and drain on paper towels (discard any scorched bits). Serve warm, piled in a napkin-lined basket or on a plate; sprinkle with salt. Or let cool completely, package airtight, and refrigerate for up to 3 days. To reheat, spread in a single layer in a shallow pan and heat in a 350° oven for 2 to 3 minutes. Makes about 6 cups.

Marinated Baby Carrots

About 1 pound baby carrots
Boiling water
2 bay leaves
½ cup distilled white vinegar

¼ cup water
3 tablespoons sugar
½ teaspoon *each* salt, mustard seeds, and dill weed

¼ teaspoon *each* crushed red pepper and dill seeds
1 clove garlic, minced or pressed

Petite size, inherent sweetness, and tender-crisp texture make these miniature carrots an appetizing, as well as low-calorie, snack. Prepare them well ahead so they'll have plenty of time to marinate.

*A*rrange whole carrots in a vegetable steamer. Cover and steam over boiling water until just tender when pierced (10 to 12 minutes). Plunge into cold water to cool quickly; then drain.

Pack carrots in a clean pint jar; tuck in bay leaves. In a bowl, stir together vinegar, water, sugar, salt, mustard seeds, dill weed, red pepper, dill seeds, and garlic until sugar is dissolved. Pour over carrots, cover, and refrigerate for at least 2 days or up to 3 weeks. Makes 1 pint.

Hot Pickled Cauliflower

1 large clove garlic
5 or 6 small dried whole hot red chiles
1½ teaspoons pickling spice
¾ pound carrots (about 4 medium size)

1 large onion
1 medium-size green pepper
1 large head cauliflower (about 2 lbs.)

3 cups water
1¼ cups white wine vinegar
2 tablespoons salt

Fiery morsels of cauliflower, green pepper, onion, and carrots speared with wooden picks make a bright and tempting offering. You'll need to prepare the vegetable mélange at least 2 weeks ahead so it has time to stand; refrigerated, it will keep almost indefinitely.

*P*eel and crush garlic (but leave whole); drop into a half-gallon jar. Break each chile in half and drop into jar. Spoon in pickling spice.

Cut carrots lengthwise into quarters, then into 2-inch pieces. Cut onion and green pepper into 1-inch squares. Break cauliflower into flowerets.

Distribute vegetables in jar, making 2 or 3 layers of each and packing as tightly as possible. Bring water, vinegar, and salt to a boil; then pour over vegetables. Cover, cool, and refrigerate for at least 2 weeks before sampling. Makes about 2 quarts.

Garlic Olives

3 tablespoons olive oil
1 clove garlic, minced or pressed
½ teaspoon oregano leaves

2 cans (7 oz. *each*) pitted ripe olives, drained

Easy to make, these tasty Italian-style olives should be prepared at least 4 hours in advance so the olives will have enough time to soak up the marinade.

*I*n a small bowl, stir together oil, garlic, and oregano. Add olives and toss to coat thoroughly with marinade. Cover and refrigerate for at least 4 hours or up to 2 weeks. Makes about 1½ cups.

Begin a glittering evening with an
appetizer assortment of sizzling Ham & Papaya Pupus
(page 57), Pork Rillettes (page 19) to spread on French bread, and
crisp, caramelized Candied Pecans (page 5).

Cherry Tomatoes with Smoked Oysters

2 baskets cherry tomatoes
1 can (3 oz.) tiny smoked oysters, drained

The unusual flavor combination of these colorful fresh tomato and smoked oyster appetizers is sure to bring raves from your guests; and you'll appreciate their ease of preparation.

*R*emove stems from tomatoes. Slice each tomato vertically to within about ¼ inch of base; spread apart and slip in a smoked oyster. Makes about 40 appetizers.

Chèvre & Green Grapes

Pictured on page 10

2 ounces (¼ cup) soft unripened plain goat cheese (such as Montrachet)
¼ to ½ teaspoon whipping cream or milk (optional)
20 large seedless grapes
⅓ cup minced roasted pistachios

Coat seedless grapes with tangy whipped goat cheese, roll in minced pistachios, then cut in half and arrange on a serving tray or plate for a refreshing and colorful nibble.

*W*ith an electric mixer, beat cheese until smooth, adding cream, if needed. Pat about ½ teaspoon of the cheese evenly around each grape. Place on a flat plate or pan in a single layer; cover and refrigerate until firm (about 2 hours) or for up to a day.

Roll grapes in pistachios. With a sharp knife, gently cut grapes in half, taking care not to crumble cheese. Arrange cut side up on a tray. If made ahead, cover and refrigerate for up to 3 hours. Makes 40 appetizers.

Belgian Endive with Cheese

Pictured on page 10

About 6 ounces Belgian endive (3 medium-size or 2 large heads)
¼ small red or green bell pepper
About 4 ounces (½ cup) soft unripened plain goat cheese (such as Montrachet) or cream cheese with herbs
1 to 2 teaspoons whipping cream or milk (optional)
20 whole chives or tiny fresh dill sprigs

Use a pastry bag to pipe curly ribbons of softened goat cheese into crisp endive leaves. Chives and red pepper spears add color.

*C*ut 20 outer leaves from endive; reserve remainder for salads. Rinse leaves; then wrap in a paper towel, enclose in a plastic bag, and refrigerate for at least 2 hours or up to a day.

Cut twenty ¼ by 1-inch strips of bell pepper. If made ahead, wrap in a damp paper towel, enclose in a plastic bag, and refrigerate for up to a day.

With an electric mixer, beat cheese until smooth, adding cream, if needed. Using a pastry bag fitted with a plain or rosette tip (about ⅜ in.), pipe about 2 teaspoons of the cheese into wide end of each endive leaf (or use a spoon instead of pastry bag). Garnish each with a bell pepper piece and a chive. If made ahead, cover and refrigerate for up to 3 hours. Makes 20 appetizers.

Planning an All-Appetizer Party

The most successful parties, large or small, have one happy similarity—both guests and hosts feel comfortable and relaxed. An all-appetizer party, where much of the food can be prepared ahead and set out with little need for attention, can be especially enjoyable. But as for any party, good planning is crucial.

Here are some guidelines to help you decide what to serve, how much you'll need, how to arrange your offerings, and how to manage your time. For actual menu suggestions and themes, see page 93.

Variety in Concert

One factor to consider in selecting the foods is to serve an appealing contrast of hot and cold appetizers. As you plan, you'll need to weigh such practical matters as how much space is available in your refrigerator or freezer—and how many appetizers you can heat at one time.

Foods served together should also offer different textures—crisp, crunchy vegetables and crackers match up agreeably with creamy dips or cheeses. Think about flavor variety, as well. No matter how much you like garlic, an hors d'oeuvre assortment in which garlic seasons every dish would be monotonous. Apparent lightness or richness counts, too. Oppose spicy, dense, or richly flavored foods, such as a buttery pâté, with something fresh and uncomplicated, like ice-cold radishes.

For variety at a large party, plan on serving at least one appetizer from each of these categories: meat or poultry, fish or seafood, cheese, and vegetables or fruits. You'll want a good balance for a small gathering, too, but on a less ambitious scale.

Eye appeal is always important for party appetizers. No matter how attractive foods are individually, you must also consider their collective impact. Make sure the colors of foods served side by side contrast appealingly. Add bright accents to perk up somber or monochromatic dishes. A glance at the photographs and garnishing suggestions in these pages will give you a good start.

How Much Food?

Unfortunately, there are no hard and fast answers for every party. Weather matters—people tend to eat more when it's cold and drink more when it's hot. Time of day is also influential. You can probably plan on slightly less food for a mid-afternoon party than for an early evening one.

For foods that are passed on trays, prepare at least two of each kind of hors d'oeuvre per person and serve at least six different appetizers of this type each hour. Supplement them with foods that guests can help themselves to, such as dips, spreads, and cheeses.

Using Space Effectively

How you place foods depends largely on space. In some rooms, the only choice is to arrange foods on a buffet table. But you can encourage socializing and give your party greater flexibility if you use small tables at various points in one or more rooms, including outdoor areas when weather permits.

When you serve appetizers buffet style, choose foods that are for the most part easy to pick up quickly. Too many offerings that must be spooned out, sliced, or spread laboriously tend to cause people to bunch up. If you can, move a buffet table away from a wall so guests can circulate around it.

Budgeting Your Time

Unless you work well under pressure, do your shopping—for both food and serving needs—well in advance and prepare as many dishes ahead as possible. When you freeze appetizers, use specially designed freezer wraps and containers. And follow the recipe guidelines as to how long to store foods in the refrigerator or freezer so they'll be at their best when you're ready to serve them.

Remember that *you* are part of your party's atmosphere. Too many dishes that require last-minute attention will keep you in the kitchen instead of with your guests. When you're sure that every detail is manageable, you'll have more fun, and so will everyone else.

Shapely finger foods—Cucumber with
Golden Caviar (page 11), Beef with Pea Pods (page 11),
Chèvre & Green Grapes (page 8), and Belgian Endive with Cheese (page 8)
—vie for attention on this festive tray.

Cucumber with Golden Caviar

Pictured on facing page

2 **Japanese cucumbers or 1 long,
    slender English cucumber**
¼ **to ⅓ cup sour cream**

¼ **to ⅓ cup golden whitefish caviar
    or other caviar**
Lime juice

Tulip-shaped cucumber cups flaunt centers of shimmering caviar over sour cream.

Cut stem end of cucumber flat. Hold vertically; 1½ inches up from flat end, insert knife tip at a 45° angle and, rotating cucumber, make 3 equally spaced cuts to center. Pull to release cup.

Trim pointed end flat and repeat cuts to make a total of 16 cups. If made ahead, cover and refrigerate for up to 2 days.

Spoon ½ to 1 teaspoon of the sour cream into each cucumber cup. Top with ½ to 1 teaspoon of the caviar. Sprinkle a little lime juice over caviar. Makes 16 appetizers.

Glazed Shrimp Crisps

**About ½ English cucumber, peeled
Glazed Shrimp (recipe follows)**

**About 1 teaspoon red salmon
    caviar or other caviar**

Finely chopped parsley

Crisp cucumber rounds stand in for bread as the foundation of these glazed shrimp canapés, garnished with caviar.

Cut 12 cucumber rounds, each ¼ inch thick. Prepare Glazed Shrimp and distribute evenly over each round. Garnish each with a few beads of caviar and a sprinkling of parsley. If made

ahead, cover and refrigerate for up to 2 hours. Makes a dozen appetizers.

Glazed Shrimp. In a small bowl, stir together ¼ pound **small cooked shrimp,** 2 teaspoons **mayonnaise,** ½ teaspoon **Dijon mustard,** and ⅛ teaspoon **white pepper.** If made ahead, cover and refrigerate for up to a day.

Beef with Pea Pods

Pictured on facing page

10 **large Chinese pea pods
    Boiling water**

10 **ounces cold rare-cooked, tender
    beef (fillet or rib)**

Horseradish Dip (recipe follows)

Barely cooked Chinese pea pods (also called snow peas) enclose juicy morsels of rare roast beef. Offer with a small bowl of zesty horseradish-flavored dip.

Remove ends and strings from pea pods. Immerse pea pods in boiling water and cook, uncovered, until bright green (about 30 seconds). Drain and immerse in cold water; when cool, drain again. Separate pod halves. If made ahead, cover and refrigerate for up to a day.

Trim fat from beef and slice thinly into 20 equal portions; roll each up. Wrap a pod half around each beef roll and secure with a wooden pick. If made ahead, cover and refrigerate for up to 6 hours. Prepare Horseradish Dip and serve with beef rolls. Makes 20 appetizers.

Horseradish Dip. In a small bowl, blend ¼ cup **sour cream,** 1½ teaspoons **prepared horseradish,** and **salt** to taste. If made ahead, cover and refrigerate for up to a day. Makes about ⅓ cup.

Dips, Spreads & Pâtés

E fficient party-givers depend on dips, spreads, and pâtés. Many can be made ahead and refrigerated, ready to be whisked to the table as the first guest arrives. And without much more attention, they last throughout the party.

Choose from a wide assortment of dips—savory, light and wholesome, or richly creamy. Many of the cold ones pair up as perfectly with fresh, crisp vegetables as with the more traditional chips or crackers.

Nothing is more eye-catching on a party buffet than cheese presented dramatically or thin slices of pâté made of artfully blended seafood or vegetables. These, too, provide popular party sustenance with make-ahead convenience.

Sugar Snap Peas with Mint Sauce

Pictured on page 15

1 **pound sugar snap peas**
¼ **cup** *each* **sour cream and mayonnaise**

2 **tablespoons fresh mint leaves**
3 **to 4 cups cubed or cracked ice**

Slivered mint leaves

Arrange sweet sugar snap peas on a bed of ice.

*U*se your fingers to snap off (or a knife to trim) top and bottom ends of peas, pulling strings away from both sides. Bring 1 to 2 inches water to a boil in a 10 to 12-inch frying pan over high heat. Add peas and cook, uncovered, until bright green (about 30 seconds). Drain peas and immerse in ice water; stir gently until cool. Drain. If made ahead, cover and refrigerate for up to a day.

In a food processor or blender, whirl sour cream, mayonnaise, and the 2 tablespoons mint until mint is finely chopped. If made ahead, cover and refrigerate for up to a day.

To serve, arrange peas on a bed of ice on a rimmed serving platter. Pour mint dip into a small bowl and nest in ice. Garnish dip with slivered mint leaves. Makes 5 or 6 servings.

Italian Eggplant Relish

Pictured on page 18

1 **large eggplant (about 1½ lbs.)**
2 **large red bell peppers**
½ **cup olive oil**
1 **large onion, finely chopped**
1½ **cups thinly sliced celery**

3 **cloves garlic, minced or pressed**
¼ **cup tomato paste**
1 **cup water**
¼ **cup red wine vinegar**
1 **tablespoon** *each* **sugar and drained capers**

2 **tablespoons coarsely chopped fresh basil or 1 teaspoon dry basil**
1 **cup sliced ripe olives**
¼ **cup pine nuts**

Scoop this dip up with lettuce leaves or Parmesan Pocket Bread Appetizers (page 33).

*C*ut unpeeled eggplant into ½-inch cubes. Core, seed, and dice peppers; set aside. Heat oil in a 12 to 14-inch frying pan over medium heat. Add eggplant; cover and cook, stirring occasionally, until slightly soft (about 5 minutes). Uncover and continue cooking, stirring often, until eggplant begins to brown (about 10 more minutes).

Mix in peppers, onion, celery, and garlic; cook until onion is soft (6 to 8 more minutes). Add tomato paste, water, vinegar, sugar, capers, basil, and olives. Cook, stirring often, until sauce is very thick (about 10 more minutes). If made ahead, refrigerate for up to a week.

Place nuts in a small frying pan over medium heat. Cook, stirring often, until lightly browned (about 5 minutes). Sprinkle over relish. Serve cold or at room temperature. Makes 1½ quarts.

Green Goddess Dip

1 **clove garlic, minced or pressed**
¼ **cup** *each* **coarsely chopped parsley, green onions (including tops), and watercress**

½ **teaspoon onion salt**
1 **teaspoon** *each* **dry tarragon and anchovy paste**

2 **teaspoons lemon juice**
½ **cup** *each* **mayonnaise and sour cream**

The classic salad dressing, Green Goddess, can double as a delicious change-of-pace dip for raw vegetables. It's especially good with small whole mushrooms, cherry tomatoes, and spears of romaine lettuce.

*I*n a blender or food processor, combine garlic, parsley, green onions, watercress, onion salt, tarragon, anchovy paste, and lemon juice; whirl until smooth. Stir in mayonnaise and sour cream until well combined. Makes about 1½ cups.

Red Bell Pepper Dip

Pictured on page 23

⅓ cup butter or margarine

4 large red bell peppers (1½ to 1¾ lbs. *total*), seeded and chopped (cut 2 rings and reserve for garnish)

1 small onion, finely chopped

1 clove garlic, minced or pressed

¼ teaspoon ground cumin

Dash of ground red pepper (cayenne)

1 tablespoon lemon juice

1 teaspoon *each* salt and grated lemon peel

2 teaspoons unflavored gelatin

¼ cup dry vermouth

½ cup whipping cream

6 to 8 medium-size heads Belgian endive, separated into leaves

An enticingly seasoned purée of sweet red bell peppers is surrounded by crisp endive spears.

Melt butter in a 3-quart pan over medium heat. Add bell peppers and onion; cook, stirring occasionally, until soft (about 15 minutes). Add garlic, cumin, and ground red pepper; cook for 1 more minute.

Transfer mixture to a food processor or blender. Add lemon juice and salt and whirl until smooth (you should have about 2⅔ cups). Place in a large bowl and blend in lemon peel.

In a small pan, combine gelatin and vermouth; let stand for about 5 minutes. Stir over medium heat until gelatin is dissolved. Stir into vegetable mixture. Refrigerate or place in a larger bowl of ice water, stirring occasionally, until mixture begins to set (30 to 45 minutes).

Whip cream until stiff; fold into vegetable mixture. Cover and refrigerate for at least 2 hours or up to a day. Line a 5 to 6-cup soufflé dish with endive spears. Spoon in vegetable mixture. Garnish with red pepper rings. Serve with remaining endive. Makes about 4 cups.

Spinach Dip

Pictured on page 95

1 package (10 oz.) frozen chopped spinach, thawed, or about 1 cup chopped cooked spinach

⅓ cup coarsely chopped green onions (including tops)

½ cup lightly packed parsley sprigs

1 tablespoon lemon juice

½ pint (1 cup) sour cream

1½ teaspoons pepper

2 cloves garlic, minced or pressed

Salt

About 6 cups raw vegetables, such as carrot, celery, and red bell pepper strips, turnip slices, and whole cherry tomatoes

While the barbecue coals heat, munch on fresh vegetables dunked in this peppery dip.

Drain spinach; then squeeze out as much liquid as possible. Place in a blender or food processor and add green onions, parsley, lemon juice, sour cream, pepper, and garlic. Whirl until blended. Season to taste with salt. Cover and refrigerate for at least 2 hours or up to a day. Arrange vegetables and offer with dip. Makes 2 cups.

Curry Dip

½ cup sour cream

3 tablespoons mayonnaise

½ teaspoon curry powder (or to taste)

⅛ teaspoon ground red pepper (cayenne)

1 tablespoon catsup

¼ teaspoon Worcestershire

Dash of salt

1 clove garlic, minced or pressed

The amount of curry you use to spice this dip will determine if it's meek and mild or aggressively adventurous. Offer it alongside cold cooked artichokes or an assortment of crisp raw vegetables.

Stir together sour cream, mayonnaise, curry powder, red pepper, catsup, Worcestershire, salt, and garlic until blended. Cover and refrigerate for at least 4 hours or up to a day. Stir before serving. Makes about ¾ cup.

One of the newest additions to the
garden, ice-cold sugar snap peas bring both sweetness and
crunch to a creamy, minted dip. Directions for preparing these edible-pod peas
and the accompanying dip appear on page 13.

Guacamole

2 large ripe avocados
2 to 3 tablespoons lemon or lime juice
About ½ teaspoon salt

2 to 4 canned green chiles, seeded and chopped, *or* several drops liquid hot pepper seasoning

This creamy avocado dip has almost as many variations as it has admirers.

Cut avocados in half, remove pits, and scoop out pulp. Coarsely mash with a fork. Stir in lemon juice, salt, and chiles. (Or, for a smooth dip, whirl in a food processor or blender.) Makes about 1⅔ cups.

Variations. Add one or more of the following: 1 clove **garlic,** minced or pressed, or 2 to 3 tablespoons minced onion (or use both); ½ teaspoon **ground coriander** or 2 teaspoons minced fresh coriander (cilantro); 1 **pimento,** chopped, or ½ to 1 tomato, chopped; **tomato wedges** and **fresh coriander (cilantro)** or parsley sprigs for garnish, or sprinkle with pomegranate seeds.

Smoked Salmon Mayonnaise

3 ounces smoked salmon or lox, coarsely chopped
1 egg yolk

1½ tablespoons lemon juice
3 tablespoons salad oil

1 cucumber, thinly sliced
Thin lemon slices

To extend the rich flavor of smoked salmon, blend it with egg and oil to make a mayonnaise-textured dip. Spoon it over cucumber slices or pumpernickel bread triangles.

In a food processor or blender, combine smoked salmon, egg yolk, and lemon juice; whirl until smooth. With motor running, add oil in a thin, steady stream, mixing until smoothly blended. Cover and refrigerate for at least 1 hour or up to a day.

Mound dip in a bowl. Surround with cucumber slices and garnish with lemon slices. Makes about ⅔ cup.

Shrimp Dip

1 large package (8 oz.) cream cheese, softened
¼ cup sour cream
1 tablespoon lemon juice

3 tablespoons thinly sliced green onions (including tops)
¼ to ½ teaspoon crushed red pepper
1 tablespoon milk

½ pound small cooked shrimp
Salt
1 to 2 tablespoons toasted slivered almonds

What's more festive than a rich and creamy shellfish dip to start off a springtime dinner party?

Take your choice of shrimp or crab (see the variation below) for the dip and surround it with an artfully arranged platter of cut-up vegetables, such as cauliflowerets, zucchini rounds, carrot and celery sticks, red and green bell pepper strips, jicama spears, and cherry tomatoes.

Beat together cream cheese and sour cream until smooth and fluffy. Stir in lemon juice, green onions, red pepper, milk, and shrimp (reserve a few for garnish). Season to taste with salt. Cover and refrigerate for 2 to 4 hours.

Just before serving, stir gently, turn into a serving dish, and top with reserved shrimp and almonds. Makes about 2 cups.

Pacific Crab Dip

Prepare **Shrimp Dip** (see above), omitting red pepper and shrimp; instead, use 1 small clove **garlic,** minced or pressed, and ½ pound **crab meat,** flaked. Makes about 2 cups.

Brie Fondue

Pine Nut Breadsticks (page 38) or packaged breadsticks
1 whole (2 lbs.) firm Brie cheese

Red or green bell pepper strips

For a delectable, no-fuss fondue, melt Brie cheese in a chafing dish to scoop up with breadsticks and pepper strips.

*P*repare Pine Nut Breadsticks. If made ahead, store airtight for up to 3 days or freeze.

Place whole cheese in top of a 9 to 10-inch chafing dish. Set over simmering water. Heat, stirring occasionally, until melted (15 to 20 minutes). Turn flame to medium-low. Serve with breadsticks and pepper strips for scooping up cheese. Makes 18 to 20 servings.

Hot Artichoke-Cheese Dip

Crisp-fried Tortilla Pieces page 21)
1 can (8½ oz.) artichoke hearts (packed in water), drained

1 jar (6 oz.) marinated artichoke hearts, drained
1 can (4 oz.) diced green chiles

6 tablespoons mayonnaise
1½ to 2 cups (6 to 8 oz.) shredded Cheddar cheese

For an appetizer with a Mexican accent, combine artichokes, chiles, and cheese to make this quickly prepared hot dip. Bake the dip in an attractive ovenproof dish; when it's bubbly, set the dip on a warming tray so the cheese will stay soft. Offer tortilla pieces or packaged tortilla chips for scooping up the spicy mélange.

*P*repare Crisp-fried Tortilla Pieces. Set aside. Chop all artichokes. Stir together and distribute in a well-greased 7½ by 11½-inch shallow baking dish. Scatter chiles on top; then carefully spread mayonnaise over all. Sprinkle with cheese. (At this point, you may cover and refrigerate for up to a day.)

Bake in a 350° oven, covered, for about 15 minutes (about 30 minutes if refrigerated) or until hot and bubbly. Serve hot. Place tortilla pieces in a large bowl and offer with dip. Makes 2½ cups.

Melted Cheese & Chorizo Appetizer

½ pound chorizo sausage
6 to 8 small (7 to 9-inch) flour tortillas

3 cups (12 oz.) diced jack cheese

Tear soft, warm flour tortillas into small pieces to enclose this oven-melted cheese and sausage combination. If you wish, you can set the casserole dish on a warming tray to keep the cheese mixture hot.

*R*emove casings and crumble sausage into a medium-size frying pan. Cook over medium heat, stirring often, until browned (5 to 8 minutes). Drain on paper towels; then spread in a shallow 4 to 6-cup casserole.

Wrap stack of tortillas in foil. Place in a 400° oven for 5 minutes. Meanwhile, distribute cheese over sausage in casserole. Place casserole in oven with tortillas and bake, uncovered, for 10 to 12 minutes or until cheese is melted and bubbling. Serve cheese mixture hot to spoon into warm tortillas. Makes 6 to 8 servings.

Scoop up chunks of this flavorful
Italian Eggplant Relish (page 13) with crispy triangles
of Parmesan Pocket Bread Appetizers (page 33). The generous relish recipe
makes enough for a large gathering.

18   Dips, Spreads & Pâtés

Pork Rillettes

Pictured on page 7

3 pounds boneless lean pork (shoulder, butt, or loin end)
1 teaspoon *each* salt and pepper
1 clove garlic, minced or pressed

½ teaspoon thyme leaves
1 bay leaf
½ cup *each* dry white wine and water

½ cup (¼ lb.) unsalted butter or margarine, softened
Chopped parsley

French in origin, this savory spread (pronounce it ree-YET) is good on crusty French bread accompanied by tiny, tart pickles.

*C*ut pork into 1½-inch cubes. Place meat in a 4 to 5-quart casserole or kettle and add salt, pepper, garlic, thyme, bay leaf, wine, and water. Cover tightly and bake in a 250° oven for about 4 hours or until meat is so tender it falls apart in shreds when prodded with a fork.

Discard bay leaf. Drain and reserve juices. Let meat cool; then with your fingers or 2 forks, shred pork. Let juices cool, then skim and discard fat. With a heavy spoon or your hands, combine meat, juices, and butter until well blended. Add more salt to taste, if desired. Spoon into a 5-cup crock or terrine or into individual 1-cup crocks. Serve at room temperature; sprinkle with parsley before serving. Makes about 5 cups.

Creamy Braunschweiger Appetizer

Pictured on page 95

½ pound braunschweiger or other liver sausage
½ pint (1 cup) sour cream
1 teaspoon Worcestershire

5 or 6 green onions (including tops), chopped
⅓ cup chopped parsley

3 drops liquid hot pepper seasoning
2 to 3 tablespoons prepared horseradish

Spread this pâté-like appetizer on crackers or scoop it up with raw vegetables such as celery and carrot sticks and mushrooms.

*D*iscard casing from braunschweiger, then cut sausage into chunks. In a food processor, whirl together braunschweiger, sour cream, Worcestershire, green onions, parsley, hot pepper seasoning, and horseradish until smooth and creamy. (Or beat with an electric mixer.) Cover and refrigerate for at least 4 hours or up to 2 days. Makes 2½ cups.

Rumaki Spread

½ cup (¼ lb.) butter or margarine
½ pound chicken livers
1 tablespoon soy sauce
½ teaspoon *each* onion salt and dry mustard

¼ teaspoon ground nutmeg
Dash of ground red pepper (cayenne)
1 can (5 oz.) water chestnuts, well drained and finely chopped

6 strips bacon, crisply cooked, drained, and crumbled
Thinly sliced green onions (including tops)

The flavors of the popular Japanese hot appetizer, *rumaki*, shine forth in this chicken liver spread. Crisp bacon and water chestnuts make it crunchy.

*I*n a wide frying pan over medium heat, melt butter. Add chicken livers and cook, stirring, until firm but still slightly pink inside (cut to test). Put liver mixture, soy, onion salt, mustard, nutmeg, and red pepper in a food processor or blender; whirl until smooth, stirring as needed. Stir in water chestnuts and bacon. Cover and refrigerate for at least 2 hours or up to a day.

For easy spreading, let stand at room temperature for at least an hour before serving. Garnish with green onions. Makes about 1½ cups.

Chèvre—Versatile Goat Cheese

Making cheese from goat's milk is nothing new, but the great variety of *chèvre* (the French word for goat and also for goat cheese) now available is good news for cheese enthusiasts. If you're just getting acquainted with these distinctive cheeses, here are some tips to help you choose them.

Though the majority come from France, the popularity of chèvre has stimulated domestic production. All goat cheeses have a unique tang and earthy flavor and aroma when young, and grow more robust in flavor as they age.

Like other cheeses, they can be classified as unripened (fresh) or ripened. In texture, goat cheeses can be soft, semisoft, firm, or hard.

Most of the chèvre produced domestically is categorized as *soft unripened goat cheese*. This group also includes such French varieties as Montrachet and Lezay; *crottin* is usually an unripened cheese. These cheeses vary in moisture content—some can be scooped up with a spoon, but most are firm enough to be cut with a knife.

Soft ripened goat cheeses usually have a velvety-looking, edible white surface mold, like cow's milk Brie. In this group you'll find fat logs of French bûcheron and cheeses such as Chevrita, goat milk Camembert, and chèvrefeuille, all of which ripen like Camembert—they're ready to eat when the center is creamy.

Ripened cheeses have a more complex flavor and aroma than the unripened ones; ask for a taste from one of the larger cheeses sold by the piece or use your nose to judge a small, whole cheese. Sometimes you'll see goat cheeses coated with ash, herbs, or carotene. These edible additions contribute flavor and color and inhibit the growth of surface bacteria.

Many appetizer recipes take advantage of the versatility of goat cheese. Chèvre & Green Grapes (page 8) is light and very easy to make. Or try chèvre with greens, as in Salad with Goat Cheese Dressing (page 80).

Here are a few more recipes that use chèvre to good advantage.

Chèvre in Olive Oil

About 1½ cups olive oil
¾ pound log-shaped soft unripened chèvre (plain or with any coating trimmed off), cut into 1-inch-thick slices
6 sprigs dry thyme, *each about 3 inches long*, or 1 tablespoon thyme leaves
2 sprigs dry rosemary, *each about 3 inches long*, or 2 teaspoons dry rosemary
2 teaspoons whole black peppers
2 small dried whole hot red chiles
1 clove garlic
Hot toasted French bread

Pour oil into a 3-cup jar. Add chèvre, thyme, rosemary, peppers, chiles, and garlic. (If needed, add more oil to cover cheese.) Let stand at room temperature for at least a week or up to a month.

Lift out cheese, drain, and serve with bread. Makes 4 to 6 servings.

Chèvre, Apple & Basil Salad

Cider Vinaigrette Dressing (recipe follows)
6 large or 18 small fresh basil leaves
1 medium-size tart apple, cored
½ pound soft unripened chèvre (plain or with any coating trimmed off), cut into 12 rounds or triangles, *each about ¼ inch thick*
Coarsely ground pepper

Prepare Cider Vinaigrette Dressing. In centers of 6 salad plates, place 1 large or 3 small basil leaves. Cut apple into 18 wedges. Arrange 3 apple wedges and 2 chèvre pieces on each plate; spoon dressing over. Offer pepper to sprinkle over individual servings. Makes 6 servings.

Cider Vinaigrette Dressing. Blend 3 tablespoons **olive oil**, 1 tablespoon **cider vinegar**, and ½ teaspoon *each* **Dijon mustard** and finely chopped **shallot**. Season to taste with **salt**.

20 Dips, Spreads & Pâtés

Super Nachos

½ pound *each* lean ground beef and chorizo sausage, casings removed (or use only lean ground beef—1 lb. *total*)

1 large onion, chopped

Salt

Liquid hot pepper seasoning

1 or 2 cans (about 1 lb. *each*) refried beans

1 can (4 oz.) whole green chiles (for mildest flavor, remove seeds and pith), chopped

2 to 3 cups (8 to 12 oz.) shredded jack or mild Cheddar cheese

¾ cup prepared green or red taco sauce

Crisp-fried Tortilla Pieces (recipe follows) or packaged tortilla chips

Garnishes (suggestions follow)

Presented with all its garnishes, hearty Super Nachos can serve as an appetizer for a dozen or more, or as a casual meal for 4 to 6 people.

Crumble ground beef and sausage into a wide frying pan. Add onion and cook over medium-high heat, stirring, until meat is lightly browned. Discard fat; season to taste with salt and hot pepper seasoning.

Spread beans in a shallow 10 by 15-inch baking pan or dish. Top evenly with meat mixture. Sprinkle with chiles, cover evenly with cheese, and drizzle with taco sauce. (At this point, you may cover and refrigerate for up to a day.)

Bake, uncovered, in a 400° oven for 20 to 25 minutes or until very hot throughout. Meanwhile, prepare Crisp-fried Tortilla Pieces and garnishes of your choice.

Remove pan from oven and quickly garnish, mounding avocado dip and sour cream, if used, in center and adding other garnishes as desired. Tuck tortilla pieces just around edges of bean mixture (making a petaled flower effect) and

serve immediately. If desired, keep pan hot on a warming tray. Makes 10 to 12 servings.

Crisp-fried Tortilla Pieces. Arrange 12 **corn tortillas** in a stack and cut into 6 equal wedges. Pour **salad oil** to a depth of about ½ inch into a deep 2 to 3-quart pan over medium-high heat. When oil is hot (350° to 375° on a deep-frying thermometer), add tortilla pieces, a stack at a time, stirring to separate. Cook until crisp (1 to 1½ minutes); lift from oil with a slotted spoon and drain on paper towels. Repeat until all are cooked. If desired, sprinkle lightly with **salt.** Store pieces airtight if made ahead. Makes about 8 cups.

Garnishes. Prepare some or all of the following: about ¼ cup chopped **green onions** (including some tops); about 1 cup **pitted ripe olives;** 1 can (about 8 oz.) frozen **avocado dip,** thawed, or 1 medium-size ripe avocado, peeled, pitted, and coarsely mashed; about ½ pint (1 cup) **sour cream;** 1 mild **red pickled pepper;** and **fresh coriander (cilantro)** or parsley sprigs.

Red Caviar Mousse

1 jar (3 to 4 oz.) red lumpfish or whitefish caviar

2 teaspoons unflavored gelatin

¼ cup dry vermouth or water

3 hard-cooked eggs

¾ cup sour cream

½ cup sliced green onions (including tops)

¼ cup lightly packed parsley sprigs

3 tablespoons mayonnaise

2 tablespoons lemon juice

1 teaspoon prepared horseradish

Only a small jar of inexpensive caviar is needed to make this elegant sour cream spread.

Empty caviar into a fine wire strainer and rinse with cold water; let drain. Set aside.

In a small pan, combine gelatin and vermouth; let stand for 5 minutes. Then place over medium heat and stir until gelatin is dissolved.

In a food processor, combine gelatin mixture, eggs, sour cream, green onions, parsley, mayon-

naise, lemon juice, and horseradish. Whirl until eggs are finely chopped. (Or mash eggs thoroughly with a fork; beat in other ingredients with an electric mixer.)

Stir in three-quarters of the caviar, reserving remainder. Pour into a 2-cup metal mold. Refrigerate for at least 3 hours or up to a day.

Dip mold to rim into very hot water just until edges begin to liquefy. Invert onto a serving dish. Garnish with reserved caviar. Makes 10 servings.

Spiced Cheese Spread

2 packages (8 oz. *each*) cream cheese, softened

4 tablespoons butter or margarine, softened

1 tablespoon milk

2 cloves garlic, minced or pressed

1 teaspoon *each* caraway seeds and paprika

2 teaspoons Dijon mustard

½ teaspoon anchovy paste or 1 finely chopped anchovy fillet

Small lettuce cups

Condiments: Sliced ripe olives, alfalfa sprouts, sliced red onion, crumbled crisp bacon, capers, sliced dill pickle

Spread this tangy cheese, a version of the Hungarian cheese called Liptauer, on cocktail-size rye or pumpernickel bread.

*I*n a large bowl, beat together cream cheese, butter, and milk until smooth. Stir in garlic, caraway seeds, paprika, mustard, and anchovy paste. Cover and refrigerate for at least 8 hours.

To serve, mound cheese spread on a serving platter and surround with small lettuce cups filled with condiments of your choice. Makes about 2¼ cups.

Stuffed Camembert Appetizer

1 whole (8 oz.) medium-ripe Camembert cheese

1 small package (3 oz.) cream cheese

1 wedge (1¼ oz.) Roquefort or other blue-veined cheese, crumbled

1 cup (4 oz.) shredded Cheddar cheese

1 small clove garlic, minced or pressed

1 teaspoon Italian herb seasoning or ¼ teaspoon *each* dry basil and oregano, rosemary, and thyme leaves

1 tablespoon chopped parsley

2 tablespoons butter or margarine, softened

¼ cup thinly sliced green onions (including tops)

Crackers or Melba toast

Here's a blend of four herb-seasoned cheeses.

*R*efrigerate Camembert until very cold (2 to 3 hours). With a sharp knife, cut around top, about ¼ inch in from edge, cutting down about ½ inch into cheese. With a spoon, carefully scoop out cheese (including top rind), leaving ¼-inch-thick shell intact. Wrap shell and refrigerate.

Bring Camembert, cream cheese, Roquefort, and Cheddar to room temperature. Beat combined cheeses with an electric mixer until smooth and creamy. Beat in garlic, herb seasoning, parsley, and butter; stir in green onions. Mound in Camembert shell. Cover and refrigerate for at least a day or up to 4 days. Let stand at room temperature for about 1 hour before serving. Offer with crackers. Makes about 2 cups.

Walnut Cheese Spread

½ cup chopped walnuts

10 pimento-stuffed green olives

1 large package (8 oz.) cream cheese, softened

2 teaspoons liquid from olives

4 green onions (including tops), chopped

3 or 4 rounds pocket bread

Arrange wedges of toasted pocket (sometimes called pita) bread around this nutty spread.

*S*pread walnuts in a shallow baking pan and bake, uncovered, in a 350° oven for 8 to 10 minutes or until lightly browned. Let cool slightly. Finely chop olives. In a bowl, beat cheese with olive liquid until fluffy. Mix in walnuts, olives, and green onions. Cover and refrigerate for at least 2 hours or up to 2 days.

Cut each bread round into 8 wedges; pull layers apart. Spread, crust sides down, in a single layer on a large baking sheet. Bake in a 350° oven for about 10 minutes or until crisply toasted; let cool.

Mound cheese spread on a platter or in a bowl; surround with toasted pocket bread. Makes 1½ cups.

 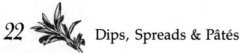 Dips, Spreads & Pâtés

Crisp spears of bitter-sweet Belgian
endive encircle Red Bell Pepper Dip (page 14), a fluffy
vegetable purée that's easily made in a food processor. Surround the dip with
additional endive spears for nibbling.

Garlic-Herb Cheese

1 large package (8 oz.) cream cheese, softened

3 tablespoons lemon juice

½ teaspoon dry or 1 teaspoon fresh winter or summer savory

¼ to ½ teaspoon freshly ground black pepper

1 clove garlic, minced or pressed

Whipping cream or milk

Reminiscent of French *boursin*, this cheese spread is spiced with savory and garlic. For a different presentation, mold it into a cone or ball and stud it with toasted nuts.

*I*n a bowl, beat cream cheese until smooth. Beat in lemon juice, savory, pepper, and garlic. If mixture seems too thick, add a little cream. Mound in a small serving bowl or press into a greased mold. Cover and refrigerate for at least 2 hours or up to 2 days. Let stand at room temperature for about 30 minutes before serving. Makes about 1¼ cups.

Nut-studded Garlic-Herb Cheese

Prepare **Garlic-Herb Cheese** (preceding); before refrigerating cheese mixture, wrap with plastic wrap, shaping mixture with your hands into a cone or ball.

Spread ½ to ⅔ cup coarsely chopped **walnuts**, slivered almonds, or whole pine nuts in a shallow baking pan. Bake, uncovered, in a 350° oven for 12 to 15 minutes or until golden brown. Let cool.

Shortly before serving, press walnuts or pine nuts over surface of cheese, or stud top and sides with almonds.

Layered Cheese Torta with Pesto

Pictured on cover

1½ pounds *each* cream cheese and unsalted butter (do not substitute margarine), softened

Pesto Filling (recipe follows)

Basil sprig

Thinly sliced French bread

Crisp raw vegetables

A dramatic-looking delicatessen newcomer is the handsome, striped Italian cheese called *torta* — alternating layers of delicate, buttery cheese and distinctively flavored seasonings. It's not difficult to make one of your own; mold the cheese in a charlotte or tall brioche mold, a loaf pan, or even a clean flowerpot. You can prepare the torta up to 5 days ahead.

*W*ith an electric mixer, beat cream cheese and butter until very smoothly blended, scraping mixture from sides of bowl as needed.

Prepare Pesto Filling. Set aside.

Cut two 18-inch squares of cheesecloth (or an 18-inch square of unbleached muslin); moisten with water, wring dry, and lay out flat, one on top of the other. Use cloth to smoothly line a 10-cup straight-sided plain mold such as a tall brioche or charlotte pan, a loaf pan, or a clean flowerpot; drape excess cloth over rim of mold.

With your fingers or a rubber spatula, spread an eighth of the cheese mixture in the prepared mold. Cover with a seventh of the filling, ex-tending it evenly to sides of mold. Repeat until mold is filled, finishing with cheese. (For thinner or thicker layers, divide cheese and filling accordingly; always have a bottom and top layer of cheese.)

Fold ends of cloth over top and press down lightly with your hands to compact. Refrigerate until torta feels firm when pressed (1 to 1½ hours); then invert onto a serving dish and gently pull off cloth (if allowed to stand longer, cloth will act as a wick and cause filling color to bleed onto cheese).

If made ahead, cover with plastic wrap and refrigerate for up to 5 days. Garnish with basil sprig and offer with bread and vegetables. Makes 20 to 25 servings.

Pesto Filling. In a blender or food processor, whirl to a paste 3¼ cups lightly packed **fresh basil leaves**, 1½ cups (4½ oz.) freshly grated **Parmesan or Romano cheese**, and ½ cup **olive oil**. Stir in 6 tablespoons (2-oz. package) **pine nuts** and season to taste with **salt** and **pepper**.

 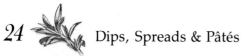

Pecan-crowned Baked Brie

1 whole (2 lbs.) firm Brie cheese
2 tablespoons butter or margarine, melted

1 cup pecan or walnut halves
Apple or pear wedges or breadsticks

Apple or pear wedges make juicy scoopers for a round of Brie, softened in the oven.

*P*lace cheese in a 10 to 11-inch round rimmed baking dish (one you can bring to the table).

Brush cheese with butter. Arrange nut halves on top. Bake in a 350° oven for 10 to 12 minutes or just until cheese begins to melt. Serve with fruit wedges for scooping up cheese. Keep hot on a warming tray. Makes 24 servings.

Sautéed Camembert

1 whole (7 to 8 oz.) firm Camembert or Brie cheese
⅓ cup fine dry bread crumbs

½ teaspoon fines herbes or thyme leaves
1 egg, beaten
3 tablespoons butter or margarine

3 tablespoons thinly sliced green onions (including tops)
Sliced French bread, toasted

The crisp crumb and herb coating of this quickly cooked Camembert conceals a fondue-like interior.

*L*et cheese stand at room temperature for about 15 minutes. Mix crumbs and fines herbes. Coat cheese with egg, then crumb mixture.

In a small frying pan over medium-low heat, melt butter. Add cheese and cook until golden on bottom (1 to 2 minutes—if cheese leaks at edges, turn immediately). Lightly brown other side (½ to 1 minute). If desired, transfer to a warm plate. Garnish with green onions and serve hot with bread. Makes 4 to 6 servings.

Black Caviar Pie

1 jar (3 to 4 oz.) black lumpfish or whitefish caviar
Mustard Eggs (recipe follows)
1 cup chopped green onions (including tops)

1 jar (2 oz.) sliced pimentos, drained
1 large package (8 oz.) cream cheese, softened
⅔ cup sour cream

Dill sprigs
Thin lemon slices
Unsalted crackers

Crown tiers of egg salad, green onions, and a rich cream cheese mixture with a flourish of black caviar for an attractive and appealing appetizer offering.

*E*mpty caviar into a fine wire strainer and rinse with cold water; let drain. Cover and refrigerate.

Prepare Mustard Eggs and spread in a 9-inch tart pan with a removable bottom. Top with green onions and pimentos. Cover and refrigerate until firm (about 1 hour).

Smoothly blend cream cheese and sour cream. Spoon about two-thirds of the mixture over green onions and pimentos. Using a pastry tube with a star tip, pipe remaining cream cheese mixture decoratively around edge. Cover loosely and refrigerate for at least 1 hour or up to a day.

Just before serving, remove sides of pan and spoon caviar into center of pie. Decorate with dill sprigs and lemon slices. Cut into thin wedges to serve with crackers. Makes 12 to 16 servings.

Mustard Eggs. In a food processor or blender, combine 6 **hard-cooked eggs**; ⅓ cup **butter** or margarine, softened; 2 teaspoons *each* **Dijon mustard** and **white wine vinegar**; and 1 tablespoon chopped **fresh dill** or 1 teaspoon dill weed. Whirl until smooth. Season with **salt.**

Shimmering aspic seals in eye-catching
decorations made from flowers, herbs, and other greenery
on an assortment of familiar cheeses—jack, gourmandise, Cheddar, and
Camembert. The instructions are on the facing page.

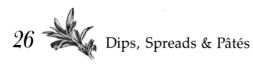

Decorated Cheese in Aspic

Like Cinderella before the ball, precut wedges of supermarket cheese are so plain that you'd hardly suspect their potential for transformation. But with the artful touch of flowers and herbs sealed beneath a shimmering transparent aspic, as pictured on the facing page, such a cheese can—like Cinderella—be the prettiest sight of the party.

The cheeses look like a caterer's specialty, but they aren't difficult to prepare. If you can make gelatin, you won't have any trouble creating these glamorous appetizers. Once you've gathered the materials, experiment with flowers and greenery to arrive at the most attractive arrangement before you make the glaze that will seal it.

After the glazing is completed, you can refrigerate the cheeses for up to 36 hours.

Choosing the cheeses. Any flat-surfaced cheese with an edible rind can be used. If you're combining several cheeses on a board or tray, select different shapes and sizes—one round, another rectangular, a wedge or triangle of a third.

You'll want to choose cheese textures that are contrasting, such as a firm, a semisoft, and a soft. Though this technique makes even your favorite jack or Cheddar look superb, a full round of ripe Brie or Camembert can also be enhanced by this treatment.

Refrigerate the cheese so it will be cold when you apply the glaze. This helps it adhere and set more quickly.

Edible decorations. Choose pesticide-free, well-washed leaves or sprigs of herbs, and petals or small blossoms of flowers. Suggested greenery includes chives, dill, sage, thyme, tarragon, rosemary, watercress, cilantro, and parsley. Just a few of the flowers you might decorate with are pansies, roses, primroses, geraniums, carnations, nasturtiums, violets, and strawberry blossoms.

After rinsing and blotting dry with paper towels, store the selection of leaves and flowers in plastic bags in the refrigerator until you're ready to garnish the cheese.

Aspic-glazed Cheese
Pictured on facing page

Here's everything you need to decorate and glaze several cheeses. Wine will give a clearer, more sparkling aspic than broth.

> 2 cups dry white wine or regular-strength chicken broth
> 1 envelope unflavored gelatin
> Flat-surfaced cheese (any rind must be edible), chilled
> Decorations (see above)

In a 2 to 3-quart pan, combine wine and gelatin; let stand for 5 minutes. Place over medium heat and stir until gelatin is completely dissolved and mixture is clear.

Place pan in a larger container filled with ice water. Stir liquid occasionally (stir slowly so bubbles don't form) until it begins to thicken and look syrupy. If aspic becomes too firm, reheat to soften, then chill again until syrupy.

Set cold cheese on a wire rack in a shallow rimmed pan. Arrange decorations on cheese to fix pattern, then remove decorations and set aside. Spoon a coat of aspic over top and sides of cheese; when slightly tacky (1 to 3 minutes), add decorations in desired pattern. Refrigerate entire pan with rack and cheese, uncovered, for about 15 minutes.

Spoon more aspic over top and sides of cheese. If necessary, add 1 or 2 more coats, refrigerating after each layer is added, in order to cover all exposed portions of decoration.

When cheese is completely covered with glaze, invert a bowl over cheese without touching surface and refrigerate until ready to serve (up to 36 hours).

Unused aspic (including drippings from under rack) can be refrigerated, covered, for several days. Reheat to melt, then chill as before over a larger container of ice water until syrupy enough to coat cheese. Makes enough to coat six 3 by 5-inch rectangles of cheese with 3 layers of aspic.

Veal & Olive Terrine

2 tablespoons butter or margarine	2 eggs	¾ pound ground veal
2 large onions, finely chopped	¼ cup fine dry bread crumbs	½ pound ground pork
2 cloves garlic, minced or pressed	1 teaspoon dry basil	3 bay leaves
30 pimento-stuffed green olives	½ teaspoon salt	
	⅛ teaspoon white pepper	

Terrine, a French word often used to describe a deep, straight-sided pan or baking dish, sometimes covered, is also one of several names given to the glorified meat loaf baked in it. Thin slices of this veal and pork terrine reveal a colorful layer of pimento-stuffed green olives.

You'll need to make the terrine at least 8 hours ahead so that its flavors have enough time to mingle. Refrigerated, it will keep for several days. Accompany it with slices of crusty French bread.

Melt butter in a 10 to 12-inch frying pan over medium heat. Add onions and cook, stirring often, until soft (8 to 10 minutes). Stir in garlic; then remove from heat and let cool slightly. Finely chop half the olives, reserving remaining olives whole.

Beat eggs in a large bowl. Mix in bread crumbs, basil, salt, and white pepper. Then add onion mixture, chopped olives, veal, and pork and mix until blended. Spread half the mixture in a deep, straight-sided 4½ to 5-cup pan or baking dish. Arrange whole olives in 2 or 3 rows down length of pan. Spread remaining meat mixture over olives. Decorate with bay leaves.

Cover and place in a larger pan. Put in a 350° oven and pour scalding water into larger pan to a depth of at least 1 inch. Bake for 1 hour and 20 to 30 minutes or until meat is firm when pressed and juices run clear when a knife is inserted in center. Let cool; then cover and refrigerate for at least 8 hours or up to 5 days.

Just before serving, remove and discard solid fat. Slice about ¼ inch thick and lift slices carefully from pan. Makes 12 to 16 servings.

Glazed Chicken Liver Pâté

Pictured on page 31

¾ pound chicken livers	¼ teaspoon *each* salt, ground nutmeg, and anchovy paste	¼ cup *each* water and condensed consommé
¾ cup (¼ lb. plus 4 tablespoons) butter or margarine	Dash *each* of ground red pepper (cayenne) and ground cloves	Lemon and carrot slices
3 tablespoons finely chopped onion	¼ teaspoon unflavored gelatin	Parsley leaves
1 teaspoon dry mustard		

Coated with a thin layer of gelatin, attractively decorated, and presented in a handsome terrine, this creamy pâté is an appetizer favorite, and for good reason. It's easy to prepare, requires no attention once it's served, and spreads smoothly on toasted French bread or Melba toast.

Place livers in a 2-quart pan and cover with water; bring to a boil over medium-high heat. Reduce heat, cover, and simmer until livers are firm but still tender when pierced with a fork (12 to 15 minutes). Let cool slightly in liquid (about 15 minutes).

Drain livers and whirl in a food processor or blender until smooth. Add butter and process until fluffy. Blend in onion, mustard, salt, nutmeg, anchovy paste, red pepper, and cloves. Spread in a 2½ to 3-cup terrine, pressing mixture in evenly; cover and refrigerate until firm (about 1 hour).

In a small pan, combine gelatin and water; let stand for 5 minutes. Add consommé and heat, stirring occasionally, until gelatin is completely dissolved. Let mixture cool to room temperature. Decorate pâté with lemon and carrot slices and parsley; then spoon gelatin evenly over top. Refrigerate until gelatin is set (at least 1 hour). If made ahead, cover after gelatin is firm and refrigerate for up to 2 days. Makes about 2½ cups.

 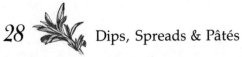

Tongue Pâté

1 pound smooth-textured liver sausage, such as braunschweiger or liverwurst, softened

¾ cup (¼ lb. plus 4 tablespoons) butter or margarine, softened

About 1 pound smoked tongue, sliced paper thin

¾ cup thinly sliced green onions (including tops)

Small sweet gherkins or dill pickles

Thinly sliced French bread

Ribbons of pink smoked tongue layered with creamy liver sausage combine attractively in this elegant-looking pâté that requires no cooking. Be sure to prepare it at least a day in advance. Refrigerated, it will keep for up to 4 days.

*R*emove casing from sausage and whirl with butter in a food processor (or beat with an electric mixer) until smoothly blended.

Line bottom and sides of a 4½ by 8-inch loaf pan with 2 layers of tongue slices, overlapping to cover bottom and sides of pan completely and allowing ends to extend over pan rim. Spread an eighth of the sausage mixture in a layer over tongue; sprinkle with a few green onions. Trim and fit enough tongue slices to make 2 more layers, covering sausage mixture and using trimmings to fill in as needed.

Repeat layers of sausage, green onions, and tongue until all ingredients are used, pressing down lightly as you work to form a firm loaf. Fold over any tongue extending beyond rim. Cover and refrigerate for at least a day or up to 4 days.

To serve, slip a knife between tongue and pan edges; firmly invert pâté to release it. Cut loaf into ¼ to ½-inch slices. Serve with gherkins and French bread. Makes 12 to 16 servings.

Baked Fish Terrine

½ pound medium-size (30 to 40 per lb.) shrimp, shelled and deveined

½ pound lean, boneless, white-fleshed fish (sole, Greenland turbot, rockfish, or halibut), cut into pieces

1 egg

⅓ cup whipping cream

½ pound salmon fillet, skinned

Hollandaise Sauce (recipe follows)

Butter lettuce leaves

A pink vein of salmon runs through the center of each slice of this delicate fish and shrimp terrine. Its elegance belies its simplicity. Arrange the slices on a lettuce-lined platter or tray, and offer them with a bowl of Hollandaise sauce alongside.

*I*n a food processor or blender, purée shrimp and white-fleshed fish; mix in egg and cream.

Spread half the fish mixture in a deep, straight-sided 1½-quart pan or baking dish. Cut salmon fillet lengthwise into 1-inch strips; arrange evenly down center of pan. Top with remaining fish mixture.

Cover and place in a larger pan. Put into a 350° oven and pour scalding water into larger pan to about half the depth of terrine pan. Bake for 40 to 50 minutes or until set when lightly touched in center. Lift out pan, uncover, and let cool. Then cover and refrigerate for at least 6 hours or up to a day.

Prepare Hollandaise Sauce. To serve terrine, arrange lettuce leaves on a serving platter. Cut terrine into about ½-inch slices, lift slices carefully from pan, and arrange on lettuce. Serve with sauce. Makes 8 to 10 servings.

Hollandaise Sauce. Melt 1 cup (½ lb.) **butter** or margarine over medium heat. In a blender or food processor, whirl 1 **egg** or 3 egg yolks, 1 teaspoon **Dijon mustard**, and 1 tablespoon **lemon juice** or white wine vinegar until well blended. With motor on high, add hot butter, a few drops at a time in the beginning, increasing to a slow, steady stream about ¹⁄₁₆ inch wide as mixture begins to thicken.

Serve immediately. Or if sauce is to be used within several hours, let stand; then reheat by placing container of sauce in water just warm to touch, mixing constantly with a fork. Transfer to water that's hot to touch; stir with a whisk until sauce is slightly warmed. Makes 1 to 1½ cups.

Sausage in Brioche

1 package active dry yeast
¼ cup warm water (about 110°)
1 tablespoon sugar
½ teaspoon salt

2 cups all-purpose flour
2 eggs
½ cup (¼ lb.) butter or margarine, softened

1 ring (1 lb.) fully cooked Polish sausage (kielbasa), cut in half
1 egg beaten with 1 teaspoon water
Dijon mustard

A rich yeast pastry encloses flavorsome Polish sausage for a savory hot appetizer.

*S*prinkle yeast over water in large bowl of an electric mixer; let stand for 5 minutes. Mix in sugar, salt, and ½ cup of the flour. Beat at medium speed until elastic (about 3 minutes). Beat in eggs, one at a time, until smooth; gradually beat in remaining 1½ cups flour. Beat in butter, 1 tablespoon at a time.

Transfer dough to a greased bowl, cover, and let rise in a warm place until doubled (about 1½ hours). Stir dough down and divide in half.

On a well-floured board, roll each half into an 8 by 12-inch rectangle. Place half the sausage on each, about 1 inch from a long edge. Roll dough over sausage and continue rolling to other side. Pinch edges. Place, sealed side down, on a greased baking sheet.

Cover and let rise until puffy (about 40 minutes) or refrigerate for up to a day; remove from refrigerator about 1 hour before baking. Brush with egg mixture. Bake in a 375° oven for 25 to 30 minutes or until well browned. Slice about ¾ inch thick; serve warm with mustard. Makes 24 to 30 servings.

Spinach-Broccoli Pâté

About ¾ pound broccoli
1½ cups water
1 medium-size onion, chopped
4 eggs

6 tablespoons all-purpose flour
Salt
Salad oil
1 pound spinach, stems removed

2 cloves garlic, minced or pressed
1 teaspoon grated lemon peel
Tarragon Mayonnaise (recipe follows)
Lemon slices

This vegetable pâté contrasts pale green broccoli purée with deep green spinach.

*T*rim broccoli ends; peel stems. Chop flowerets and enough stems to make 2 cups. Boil water in a 2 to 3-quart pan. Add broccoli and half the onion; cook, covered, over medium-high heat until broccoli is just tender (6 to 8 minutes). Drain; spread on paper towels.

Purée broccoli mixture, 2 of the eggs, and 3 tablespoons of the flour in a food processor; season to taste with salt. Oil a 5 to 6-cup terrine or loaf pan. Spread purée evenly in pan.

Rinse spinach well (you should have 6 to 6½ cups, packed). Drain but do not dry. Place spinach in a 3 to 4-quart pan; cover and cook over medium heat, stirring once or twice, until wilted (6 to 8 minutes). Transfer to a colander and press gently to remove excess moisture. In a food processor, purée spinach, remaining onion, remaining 2 eggs, remaining 3 tablespoons flour, garlic, and lemon peel. Season to taste with salt.

Spoon spinach mixture evenly over broccoli purée, taking care to preserve layers. Cover and place in a larger pan. Set in a 400° oven and pour

scalding water into larger pan to a depth of 1 inch. Bake for 1 hour and 10 to 15 minutes or until top feels firm when gently pressed in center. Uncover and let cool. If made ahead, cover and refrigerate for up to 3 days.

Prepare Tarragon Mayonnaise. Serve pâté from terrine, garnished with lemon slices. Slip a knife around pan edges, slice in 10 crosswise cuts, and lift out slices with a wide spatula. Accompany with mayonnaise. Makes 10 servings.

Tarragon Mayonnaise. In a blender or food processor, whirl 1 **egg,** 1 teaspoon **Dijon mustard,** ¼ teaspoon *each* **salt** and **dry tarragon,** and 1 teaspoon **tarragon vinegar** at high speed until well blended. Measure ¼ cup **olive oil** and ¾ cup **salad oil.** With motor running, slowly add oil, a few drops at a time in the beginning, increasing to a slow, steady stream about 1/16 inch wide as mixture begins to thicken.

When half the oil is added, add 1 more teaspoon tarragon vinegar, then continue whirling and add remaining oil. Mix in 1 more teaspoon tarragon vinegar. Cover and refrigerate until cold or for up to 10 days. Makes about 1¼ cups.

 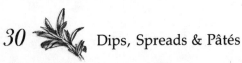

Perfect foils for the creamy richness
of this Glazed Chicken Liver Pâté (page 28) are tiny
sour pickles, nippy radishes, and toasted slices of French bread cut
from a long, narrow loaf or *baguette*.

Dips, Spreads & Pâtés

Appetizers from the Oven

*B*ring on appetizers hot from the oven, and the aroma precedes them invitingly. For that just-baked appeal, we offer a range of choices, from a simple cheese wafer to a handsome bread wreath twined around a wheel of Brie cheese.

Breads and pastries such as Cheese Twists and Tostadas de Harina lend both substance and interest to a party buffet. Artfully shaped fila dough makes bite-size appetizers, as well as the spectacular Moroccan pie, *bastilla*. Filled pastries include tiny quiches and generously proportioned savory cheesecakes.

Versatility is just one virtue of baked vegetable appetizers; serve them warm or at room temperature with equal appeal.

Parmesan Pocket Bread Appetizers

Pictured on page 18

6 rounds (10 to 12-oz. package) pocket bread

¾ cup (¼ lb. plus 4 tablespoons) butter or margarine, melted

About 1½ cups (4½ oz.) grated Parmesan cheese

Utterly simple to prepare, these crisp triangles made from pocket, or pita, bread are good on their own or for scooping up dips and spreads, such as Italian Eggplant Relish (page 13). Be sure to make plenty of these crunchy treats; they're certain to become family favorites as well as popular appetizer fare.

Cut pocket breads in half, then split each half. Brush each half with butter, sprinkle with about 1 tablespoon of the cheese, and cut into 4 wedges. Place in a single layer on ungreased baking sheets. Bake in a 350° oven for 12 to 15 minutes or until crisp and golden brown. Makes 8 dozen appetizers.

Hasty Hots

4 green onions (including tops), finely minced

½ cup grated Parmesan cheese

About 6 tablespoons mayonnaise

About 2 dozen slices cocktail-size rye bread or sliced French rolls

As the name indicates, it takes just a few minutes to put together these savory nibbles. Broil them quickly just before serving.

Stir together green onions, cheese, and mayonnaise until well blended, adding more mayon-naise, if necessary, to make a firm spreading consistency. Toast one side of bread. Spread cheese mixture on untoasted side and broil about 6 inches below heat until bubbly and lightly browned (about 3 minutes). Makes about 2 dozen appetizers.

Crab & Cheese Rounds

About 3 dozen slices cocktail-size rye bread

About 5 tablespoons butter or margarine

2 cups (about 1 lb.) cooked or canned crab meat

½ cup sour cream

1 tablespoon lemon juice

½ teaspoon Worcestershire

Dash of liquid hot pepper seasoning

1½ cups (6 oz.) shredded Swiss cheese

Paprika

Cocktail-size rye bread rounds make a handy base for many appetizer offerings. Here, the bread is toasted, buttered, and then topped with a zesty crab and cheese mixture that goes together in only a few minutes.

Bake these elegant seafood appetizers just until they're bubbly and serve them warm from the oven.

Toast bread on one side until lightly browned; spread lightly with some of the butter.

In a medium-size bowl, combine crab meat, sour cream, lemon juice, Worcestershire, hot pepper seasoning, and 1 cup of the cheese.

Spread about 1 tablespoon of the crab mixture on each slice of bread; evenly sprinkle remaining cheese on top. Then sprinkle lightly with paprika. Arrange rounds on an ungreased baking sheet.

Bake, uncovered, in a 400° oven for about 8 minutes or until hot and bubbly. Makes about 3 dozen appetizers.

Cheese enlivens these savory baked
appetizers (clockwise from top): Cheese Herb Pretzels
(page 36), Cheese Twists (page 37), Cheese Spritz (page 37), and Sesame Cheese Wafers
(page 37). French Kir (page 40) is a perfect complement.

Tostadas de Harina

6 small (7 to 9-inch) flour tortillas
2 cups (8 oz.) shredded mild
  Cheddar cheese

2 tablespoons chopped and seeded
  canned green chiles

In Mexico and the Southwest, giant-size tortillas are used to make *tostadas de harina* (crisp flour tortillas with melted cheese). But smaller, 7 to 9-inch flour tortillas work equally well; when cut into wedges, they make good appetizer-size triangles for this recipe.

For a more hearty version, you can use chorizo sausages; simply sprinkle the cooked meat over the cheese and bake the tortillas until they're browned.

*E*venly sprinkle tortillas with cheese, leaving about a ½-inch margin around edges. Top with chiles. Place on ungreased baking sheets and bake, uncovered, in a 425° oven for 8 to 10 minutes or until edges are crisp and browned. Cut each tortilla into 6 wedges. Makes 36 appetizers.

Chorizo Tostadas de Harina

Prepare **Tostadas de Harina** (see above), omitting green chiles; instead use 2 **chorizo sausages** (4 to 6 oz. *total*). Remove casings and crumble meat into a 10-inch frying pan; cook over medium heat, stirring to break up, until lightly browned. Drain meat, discarding fat. Evenly sprinkle meat over cheese-topped tortillas; then bake and cut as directed above.

Cocktail Cream Puffs

Gingered Chicken Salad (recipe
  follows)
1 cup water
½ cup (¼ lb.) butter or margarine

1 cup all-purpose flour
4 eggs

You can make the cream puff shells, tuck them into the freezer, and store them for up to a month before using them. Shortly before you're ready to serve, you recrisp the puffs briefly in the oven.

The gingery chicken salad that fills the puffs can be prepared up to a day ahead. Once the puffs are filled, you can refrigerate them for up to 2 hours before setting them out for your guests.

*P*repare Gingered Chicken Salad.

In a 3-quart pan, bring water and butter to a boil over high heat. Add flour all at once, stirring briskly until mixture leaves sides of pan and forms a ball (about 2 minutes); remove from heat. Add eggs, one at a time, beating well after each addition until dough is smooth and well blended.

On greased baking sheets, drop 1 tablespoon of the dough for each puff, spacing them about 2 inches apart. Bake in a 400° oven for 20 to 25 minutes or until well browned and crisp; cool thoroughly on wire racks.

Split puffs horizontally; pull out and discard moist portions of dough.

If made ahead, arrange puffs in a single layer and freeze until firm; then package airtight and freeze for up to a month. Before filling, arrange frozen puffs, uncovered, on baking sheets and heat in a 375° oven for 5 to 8 minutes or until centers are warm (remove top of a puff in center of baking sheet to test).

Remove tops and fill each puff with about 1 tablespoon of the filling. Replace tops and arrange on serving trays. If made ahead, refrigerate for up to 2 hours. Makes about 3 dozen appetizers.

Gingered Chicken Salad. In a medium-size bowl, smoothly blend ½ cup **mayonnaise**, ½ teaspoon **dry mustard**, and 1 teaspoon grated **fresh ginger** or ¼ teaspoon ground ginger. Add 2 cups finely chopped **cooked chicken**, ½ cup chopped and drained canned **water chestnuts**, and 2 **green onions** (including tops), thinly sliced; mix lightly to coat with mayonnaise mixture. Cover and refrigerate for at least 2 hours or up to a day.

Onion Cheese Puffs

Pictured on page 95

| ½ cup (¼ lb.) butter or margarine | 1 cup milk | 4 eggs |
| 1 large onion, finely chopped | 1 cup all-purpose flour | 1 cup (4 oz.) shredded Swiss cheese |

These cheese and onion-accented cream puffs are a miniature version of *gougère*, a traditional appetizer pastry found in the region of Burgundy, as well as elsewhere in France.

You can make the puffs ahead and freeze them. Plan on recrisping them quickly in the oven just before serving time.

*M*elt 4 tablespoons of the butter in an 8 to 10-inch frying pan over medium-low heat. Add onion and cook, stirring, until deep golden (about 25 minutes). Let cool.

In a 2 to 3-quart pan over medium heat, bring milk and remaining 4 tablespoons butter to a boil. Add flour all at once, stirring briskly until mixture leaves sides of pan and forms a ball (about 2 minutes); remove from heat.

Add eggs, one at a time, beating well after each addition until dough is smooth and well blended. Stir in onion mixture and ½ cup of the cheese.

Drop by spoonfuls, making balls about 1½ inches in diameter, on greased baking sheets. Sprinkle remaining ½ cup cheese evenly over puffs.

Bake in a 350° oven for 25 to 30 minutes or until puffed and browned. Turn off oven. Remove puffs from oven, pierce each in several places with a fork, and return to closed oven for 10 minutes to dry. Serve warm.

If made ahead, let cool completely, package airtight, and freeze for up to a month. Arrange frozen puffs, uncovered, on baking sheets and heat in a 350° oven for 5 to 7 minutes or until heated through. Makes about 3 dozen appetizers.

Cheese Herb Pretzels

Pictured on page 34

1 cup all-purpose flour	¼ teaspoon *each* dry basil, dry rosemary, and oregano leaves	1 cup (4 oz.) shredded sharp Cheddar cheese
2 tablespoons grated Parmesan cheese	½ cup (¼ lb.) butter or margarine	2 to 3 tablespoons cold water
½ teaspoon garlic powder		

Golden brown in color, flaky and light in texture, these pretzel-shaped pastries will disappear from the table in a flash. Cheddar cheese, enlivened with basil, rosemary, and oregano, provides pleasant bursts of flavor.

Offer these pretzels alone, with a glass of white wine or an apéritif, or as an accompaniment to other more hearty appetizers. They're also a perfect stand-in for the more traditional crackers when you're serving soup.

The pretzels can be made ahead, frozen, then reheated in the oven.

*I*n a large bowl, mix flour, Parmesan cheese, garlic powder, basil, rosemary, and oregano. With a pastry blender or 2 knives, cut in butter until mixture resembles fine crumbs. Stir in Cheddar cheese.

Sprinkle water, 1 tablespoon at a time, over flour mixture, mixing lightly until dough is evenly moist and clings together. With your hands, shape dough into a flattened ball. Divide in half, then cut each half into 12 equal pieces (if dough seems soft, wrap in plastic wrap and refrigerate until firm).

On a lightly floured surface, roll each piece of dough with palms of your hands into an 11-inch strand. Twist each strand into a pretzel shape and place, slightly apart, on ungreased baking sheets. Bake in a 425° oven for 12 to 15 minutes or until golden brown. Let cool on wire racks.

If made ahead, package airtight and freeze for up to a month. To recrisp, place frozen pretzels on baking sheets and heat in a 350° oven for 5 to 7 minutes. Makes 2 dozen appetizers.

Cheese Spritz

Pictured on page 34

⅔ cup butter or margarine, softened

½ cup shredded sharp Cheddar cheese

1 egg

⅛ teaspoon ground red pepper (cayenne)

¼ teaspoon dry mustard

½ teaspoon *each* salt and sugar

1⅔ cups all-purpose flour

Poppy seeds, sesame seeds, or chopped pimentos

A cooky press shapes this savory dough festively. Once shaped, you can adorn the cookies with poppy seeds, sesame seeds, or, for a splash of color, finely chopped pimentos.

In the variation following the main recipe, you form the dough into a roll like refrigerator cookies, coat it with sesame seeds, and cut wafer-thin slices.

No matter the shape, both freeze well, if made ahead.

With an electric mixer, beat together butter and cheese. Add egg, red pepper, mustard, salt, and sugar; beat until well blended. Gradually add flour, stirring until smoothly blended. With your hands, shape dough into a ball.

Put about half the dough at a time into a spritz cooky press and shape cookies on ungreased baking sheets. Sprinkle with seeds. Bake in a 375° oven for 10 to 12 minutes or until lightly browned. Serve warm or at room temperature.

If made ahead, package airtight and freeze for up to a month. Makes 2½ dozen appetizers.

Sesame Cheese Wafers

Prepare **Cheese Spritz** dough (see above), dividing dough in half and shaping each portion into a smooth log about 1½ inches in diameter. For *each* portion, sprinkle 1½ tablespoons **sesame seeds** on a board or wax paper. Roll log in seeds to coat evenly, pressing lightly to embed seeds in dough. Wrap in wax paper or plastic wrap and refrigerate until firm enough to slice easily (at least 2 hours) or for up to a day.

Slice dough about ¼ inch thick and arrange rounds slightly apart on ungreased baking sheets. Bake in a 375° oven for 10 to 12 minutes or until wafers are just firm when touched lightly and golden on bottom. Serve warm or at room temperature.

If made ahead, package airtight and freeze for up to a month. Makes about 5 dozen appetizers.

Cheese Twists

Pictured on page 34

1 cup all-purpose flour

½ teaspoon *each* salt and ground ginger

⅓ cup butter or margarine

1 cup (4 oz.) shredded sharp Cheddar cheese

½ teaspoon Worcestershire

2 to 2½ tablespoons cold water

1 egg, beaten

2 tablespoons sesame, caraway, or poppy seeds or coarse salt

When a light but elegant accompaniment to a chilled apéritif is called for, present a tray of these crisp, twisted cheese pastry strips. Crunchy sesame seeds complement their melt-in-your-mouth flakiness.

Mix flour, salt, and ginger in a large bowl. With a pastry blender or 2 knives, cut in butter until mixture resembles fine crumbs. Stir in cheese. Add Worcestershire to 1 tablespoon of the water and sprinkle over flour mixture. Mix lightly, adding more of the remaining water as needed, until dough is evenly moist and clings together. With your hands, shape dough into a flattened ball.

On a lightly floured surface, roll dough into a 10-inch square. Brush with egg and sprinkle evenly with seeds. Cut in half; then cut each half into ½-inch strips, each 5 inches long. Holding each strip at ends, twist in opposite directions.

Place about 1 inch apart on greased baking sheets. Bake in a 400° oven for 10 to 12 minutes or until golden brown. Serve warm; or let cool on wire racks and serve at room temperature. Makes 40 appetizers.

Pine Nut Breadsticks

Pictured on page 55

1 package active dry yeast
⅔ cup warm water (about 110°)
½ teaspoon anise seeds, crushed
2 tablespoons *each* salad oil and olive oil
¼ teaspoon grated lemon peel
½ teaspoon salt
1 tablespoon sugar
About 2¼ cups all-purpose flour
½ cup pine nuts
1 egg, lightly beaten
2 tablespoons coarse salt

Delicious as an unadorned nibble, with dips, or with a strip of beef twirled around each stick, this distinctively flavored appetizer is versatile indeed. Try these breadsticks with your favorite first-course soup, as well.

*I*n a large bowl, sprinkle yeast over water and let stand for 5 minutes to soften. Stir in anise seeds, salad oil, olive oil, lemon peel, salt, sugar, and 1 cup of the flour. Beat until smooth. Add pine nuts and enough of the remaining flour to make a stiff dough. Turn out onto a floured board and knead until smooth and elastic (about 5 minutes), adding more flour as needed. Place dough in a greased bowl; turn dough to grease top. Cover with plastic wrap and let rise in a warm place until doubled (about 1 hour).

Punch dough down and divide into 3 equal portions. Cut each portion into 20 equal-size pieces. With palms of your hands, roll each piece into a 6-inch-long strand. Place parallel about ½ inch apart on greased baking sheets. Cover and let rise until puffy (about 20 minutes). Brush with egg and sprinkle lightly with salt.

Bake in a 325° oven for 25 minutes or until lightly browned. Serve hot; or let cool on wire racks and serve at room temperature. Store airtight for up to 4 days or package airtight and freeze for up to a month. Makes 5 dozen appetizers.

Mini-Bagels

2 packages active dry yeast
2 cups warm water (about 110°)
3 tablespoons sugar
1 tablespoon salt
About 5¾ cups all-purpose flour
3 quarts water mixed with 1 tablespoon sugar
Cornmeal
1 egg yolk beaten with 1 tablespoon water
About 2 tablespoons poppy or sesame seeds (optional)

Bite-size bagels are luxurious topped with cream cheese and smoked salmon.

*S*prinkle yeast over warm water in large bowl of an electric mixer; let stand for 5 minutes to soften. Stir in sugar and salt. Gradually mix in 4 cups of the flour and beat at medium speed for 5 minutes. With a spoon, stir in about 1¼ cups more flour to make a stiff dough.

Turn out onto a floured board and knead until smooth, elastic, and no longer sticky (about 15 minutes); add more flour as needed to prevent sticking—dough should be firmer than for most other yeast breads. Place in a greased bowl, cover, and let rise in a warm place until almost doubled (about 40 minutes).

Punch dough down and divide into 3 equal portions. Set two-thirds of the dough aside on a floured board; cover with plastic wrap. Form remaining dough into a log and cut into 16 equal-size pieces.

To shape, knead each piece into a small ball and poke thumbs through center. With one thumb in hole (hole should be at least ½ inch), work fingers around perimeter, shaping ball into a small donutlike shape about 1½ inches in diameter. Place bagels on a floured board and let stand for 20 minutes.

Bring water mixture to a boil in a 4 to 5-quart pan; adjust heat to keep water boiling gently. Lightly grease a baking sheet and sprinkle with cornmeal. Lift bagels carefully and drop into water (about 6 at a time); boil gently for 1 minute, turning once. Lift out with a slotted spatula, drain briefly on paper towels, and place on baking sheet. Brush with a third of the egg yolk glaze, sprinkle with seeds, if desired, and bake in a 400° oven for 20 minutes or until richly browned. Let cool on wire racks.

Repeat with remaining dough (you may need to punch it down before shaping), working with half of it at a time. Makes 4 dozen appetizers.

Baked to just the size of a 2-pound
wheel of sumptuously ripe cheese, Pumpernickel Brie
Wreath (page 41) slices thinly for serving. The combination is a worthy
addition to an autumn wine-tasting party.

Spirited Liquid Refreshment

There's no "right" beverage to serve with appetizers. Instead, you can choose from a wide range, depending on the occasion, the time of day, the weather, and your taste. Here are some guidelines to help you decide what to serve and how much you'll need.

A perennial favorite with appetizers is wine. But in addition to dry and slightly off-dry white wines and light red wines, consider chilled dry sherry. It pairs well with such appetizers as seafood, eggs, and olives. Sherries labeled *fino* or *manzanilla* are light bodied, pale, and very dry; *amontillado* is only slightly sweeter.

Somewhat stronger than wine—and with added flavors to give character—are such apéritifs as Byrrh, dry or sweet vermouth, red or blonde Dubonnet, Lillet, Pineau de Charentes, Cynar, and Campari. When you serve these wine-based apéritifs, have on hand chilled club soda or mineral water, a bucket of ice, a small bowl of lemon twists or wedges, and wine or cocktail glasses. Guests can enjoy the drink as is, over ice, or with sparkling water to taste.

If you serve liquor, stock up on nonalcoholic mixers such as club soda, quinine water, orange juice, ginger ale, and cola. Sparkling mineral water is especially popular in warm weather. Over ice with an equal amount of white wine and a squeeze of lime or lemon, it makes a refreshing spritzer.

For a 2-hour party, allow about half a bottle of wine (white wine seems to have the edge in popularity over red), 8 ounces of liquor, 1 quart of beer, or 16 ounces of a mixed punch for each guest. If you're serving a nonalcoholic punch, plan on about 32 servings from one gallon. And be sure you have plenty of ice—a 5-pound bag for every 4 guests is a good estimate.

A party drink that complements ethnic appetizers can provide a gracious introduction to the carefully selected hors d'oeuvre offerings. With French food serve French Kir, made with dry white wine and crème de cassis, a black currant liqueur. Offer orange-flavored Sangría with Mexican fare. The recipes are at right.

French Kir

1 bottle (750 ml) light dry white wine (such as Chablis, white Burgundy, Chenin Blanc, or French Colombard), chilled
¼ to ½ cup crème de cassis
Lemon peel
Ice cubes (optional)

In a large pitcher, combine white wine and crème de cassis (amount depends on your own taste).

To serve, place a twist of lemon in an 8 to 10-ounce wine glass, add several ice cubes, if desired, and pour in about ½ cup of the wine mixture. Makes about 3½ cups, enough for 6 to 8 servings.

Sangría de Granada

1 medium-size orange
¼ cup sugar
2 cups orange juice
1 bottle (750 ml) dry red wine
½ cup orange-flavored liqueur
Ice cubes (optional)

Cut orange in half. Cut 1 or 2 thin slices from one half, then cut each slice in quarters and set aside.

With a vegetable peeler, cut off thin outer peel of other orange half. In a bowl, use a spoon to bruise peel with sugar to release flavorful oils; then stir in orange juice, red wine, and orange-flavored liqueur. Cover and refrigerate for about 15 minutes, then remove and discard orange peel. Return sangría to refrigerator until well chilled.

Pour sangría into a punch bowl or pitcher. Garnish with orange slices. Serve with ice, if desired. Makes about 5½ cups, enough for 10 to 12 servings.

Pumpernickel Brie Wreath

Pictured on page 39

1 package active dry yeast
1¼ cups warm water (about 110°)
¼ cup molasses
1 teaspoon salt
2 tablespoons butter or margarine, melted and cooled

1 egg, separated
¼ cup unsweetened cocoa
1 tablespoon caraway seeds
About 2 cups all-purpose flour
2¼ cups rye flour

1 tablespoon water
1 whole (about 2 lbs.) 8-inch round Brie cheese
Cluster of grapes

A braid of pumpernickel frames a round of Brie. Slice the bread thinly to spread with cheese.

*I*n large bowl of an electric mixer, sprinkle yeast over warm water; let stand for 5 minutes to soften. Stir in molasses, salt, butter, egg yolk, cocoa, and caraway seeds. With electric mixer, slowly mix in 2 cups of the all-purpose flour, scraping bowl often. Beat at medium speed for 8 minutes. With a heavy-duty mixer or wooden spoon, beat in rye flour, about ¼ cup at a time.

Turn out onto a floured board and knead until smooth (about 5 minutes), adding up to ¼ cup more all-purpose flour as needed to prevent sticking. Place dough in a greased bowl; turn to grease top. Cover and let rise in a warm place until doubled (about 1½ hours).

Meanwhile, generously grease outside of an 8-inch round cake pan and set in center of a well-greased 14 by 17-inch baking sheet or 15 to 17-inch round pizza pan.

Punch dough down, turn out, and knead on a lightly floured board until smooth. Divide into 3 equal portions. Roll each piece, one at a time (keeping others covered), into a smooth 36-inch-long strand. Place side by side on one side of cake pan. Starting in center, loosely braid strands out to each end. Wrap around pan, joining ends; pinch to seal. Cover and let rise in a warm place until almost doubled (45 minutes to 1 hour).

Beat egg white with the 1 tablespoon water; lightly brush over braid (don't let mixture accumulate around cake pan or bread may stick).

Bake in a 350° oven for about 25 minutes or until well browned. Use a knife to loosen bread around pan; then lift out pan. With a wide spatula, slide bread onto a large wire rack; let cool. If made ahead, wrap and store at room temperature for up to a day; freeze for up to a month.

To serve, place wreath on a large board or shallow basket. Cut a small section into ¼-inch slices, then fit cheese into center, spreading wreath if necessary; set slices back in place. Garnish with grapes. Makes 15 to 18 servings.

Cocktail Turnovers

Cream Cheese Pastry (recipe follows)
1 small potato (about 5 oz.)
1 small onion

½ pound lean ground beef
1 clove garlic, minced or pressed
¼ teaspoon *each* marjoram leaves and pepper

½ teaspoon oregano leaves
1 teaspoon salt
1 egg yolk beaten with 2 tablespoons milk

Fill a basket with these miniature, meat-filled triangles for an inviting light nibble. Offer them with a wine cooler or other favorite beverage.

*P*repare Cream Cheese Pastry.

Finely chop potato and onion in a food processor or by hand; combine with beef, garlic, marjoram, pepper, oregano, and salt.

On a floured board, roll pastry into a rectangle ⅛ inch thick; cut into 2½-inch squares. Place 1 teaspoon of the filling on each square. Fold dough over to make a triangle; seal edges with a fork. Brush with egg mixture. Place, slightly apart, on ungreased baking sheets. Bake in a 350° oven for about 25 minutes or until golden brown. Serve hot. Makes 4 to 5 dozen appetizers.

Cream Cheese Pastry. In a large bowl, combine 1 large package (8 oz.) **cream cheese**, softened, and 1 cup (½ lb.) **butter** or margarine, softened; beat until smooth. Beat in ½ teaspoon **salt**. Slowly mix in 2 cups **all-purpose flour** to make a stiff dough. Cover with plastic wrap and refrigerate for at least 4 hours or up to a day.

Choose either bacon and mushrooms or
ham and green chiles as a filling for tender Appetizer Mini-
Quiches (page 44). The recipe produces a generous six dozen bite-size nibbles,
but they won't last long at a party.

Appetizers from the Oven

Meat-filled Fila Triangles

1 pound lean ground beef
⅛ teaspoon *each* garlic salt and onion salt
1 can (8 oz.) tomato sauce
½ cup dry red wine
¼ cup grated Parmesan cheese
1 egg, lightly beaten
6 sheets (about 3 oz.) fila dough, thawed according to package directions, if frozen
½ cup (¼ lb.) butter or margarine, melted

Buttery morsels of flaky fila dough enclose a wine-accented meat filling.

Crumble meat into a 10 to 12-inch frying pan and cook, stirring, over medium heat until browned; drain off fat. Add garlic salt, onion salt, tomato sauce, and wine. Cook until most of the liquid has evaporated. Cover, reduce heat, and simmer for 20 minutes or until thick. Let cool slightly, then stir in cheese and egg.

Lay out fila, one sheet at a time, on a flat surface (keep remaining fila covered with plastic wrap); lightly brush with butter and cut into 3-inch lengthwise strips.

Place a heaping teaspoon of the meat filling in a corner, fold over into a triangle, and continue folding to other end, making sure filling is completely encased. Repeat entire process with remaining fila, making a total of 36 triangles.

Place about 1½ inches apart on ungreased baking sheets. Bake, uncovered, in a 375° oven for 10 minutes or until golden brown. Serve warm.

If made ahead, cool, cover, and refrigerate for up to a day; or wrap airtight and freeze for up to a month. To reheat, arrange triangles (thaw, if frozen) on baking sheets and bake, uncovered, in a 350° oven for 8 to 10 minutes or until heated through. Makes 3 dozen appetizers.

Moroccan Chicken & Egg Pastry

1 large can (49½ oz.) regular-strength chicken broth
2 medium-size onions, sliced
1 cup chopped fresh parsley
½ teaspoon salt
1 teaspoon ground ginger
¼ teaspoon pepper
1 frying chicken (about 3½ lbs.), with giblets
4 eggs
About 4 tablespoons butter or margarine, melted
4 sheets (about 2 oz.) fila dough, thawed according to package directions, if frozen
1 tablespoon granulated sugar
1 teaspoon ground cinnamon
¼ cup finely chopped blanched almonds
Powdered sugar and ground cinnamon

To open a Moroccan meal, present this savory, fila-encased chicken pie called *bastilla*.

In a large pan, combine broth, onions, parsley, salt, ginger, pepper, and chicken. Chop giblets; add to pan. Bring to a boil. Cover, reduce heat, and simmer until very tender (about 1¼ hours).

Remove chicken; strain and reserve broth. Tear meat into pieces; discard skin and bones. (At this point, you may cover and refrigerate meat and broth separately for up to a day.)

Bring broth to a boil. Lightly beat eggs, then gradually pour into broth, stirring until set (about 1 minute). Strain broth; reserve for other uses. Turn eggs into a medium-size bowl; set aside.

Brush butter over bottom and sides of a 10-inch frying pan (with sloping sides and a heatproof handle) or a 10-inch pie pan. Arrange 3 fila sheets in pan so they cover bottom and extend about 6 inches beyond pan edges all around. Sprinkle in granulated sugar, the 1 teaspoon cinnamon, and almonds. Spread chicken in pan and cover with remaining fila sheet. Spread eggs on top.

Fold fila over filling to cover completely. Brush with remaining butter. (At this point, you may cover and refrigerate for up to 4 hours.)

Bake, uncovered, in a 450° oven for about 10 minutes (about 15 minutes, if refrigerated) or until golden brown. Carefully invert onto a round platter; let stand for 5 minutes. Sift powdered sugar generously over pastry, then decorate by dusting on cinnamon in thin crisscrossed lines. Serve comfortably hot to touch. Break off pieces to eat with fingers or cut into wedges to eat with forks. Makes 8 servings.

Appetizer Mini-Quiches

Pictured on page 42

Flaky Pastry (recipe follows)
Bacon & Mushroom Filling *or*
Ham & Green Chile Filling
(recipes follow)

2 eggs
¾ cup sour cream

Baked in tiny muffin pans, these bite-size quiches can be made a day ahead, then reheated.

*P*repare Flaky Pastry. On a floured board, roll dough ¹⁄₁₆ inch thick. Cut into 2-inch circles, re-rolling scraps to make 72 circles. Fit into bottoms and part way up sides of 1¾-inch muffin cups.

Prepare either Bacon & Mushroom or Ham & Green Chile Filling. Place a heaping teaspoon of the filling into each cup. Beat eggs lightly; beat in sour cream until smooth. Spoon about 1 teaspoon of the egg mixture over filling in each cup. Bake in a 375° oven for 20 to 25 minutes or until filling puffs and tops are lightly browned. Let cool in pans for 5 minutes; remove from pans and serve warm. Or let cool on wire racks and serve at room temperature.

If made ahead, wrap airtight and refrigerate for up to a day. Reheat in a 350° oven for about 10 minutes. Makes 6 dozen appetizers.

Flaky Pastry. Mix 2 cups **all-purpose flour** and ½ teaspoon **salt.** Add either ½ teaspoon **caraway** **seeds** for Bacon & Mushroom Filling *or* ½ teaspoon **chili powder** for Ham & Green Chile Filling. With a pastry blender or 2 knives, cut in ⅓ cup *each* firm **butter** or margarine and **vegetable shortening** until mixture resembles fine crumbs. Beat 1 **egg;** add **cold water** to make ¼ cup. Add to flour mixture, 1 tablespoon at a time, mixing until dough clings together. Shape into a ball.

Bacon & Mushroom Filling. In a wide frying pan over medium heat, cook 6 strips **bacon** until crisp; drain and crumble. In same pan, melt 1 tablespoon **butter** or margarine; add ¼ pound **mushrooms,** chopped, and cook until liquid has evaporated. Mix bacon, mushrooms, ¼ cup chopped **green onions** (including tops), and 1½ cups (6 oz.) shredded **Swiss cheese.**

Ham & Green Chile Filling. In a bowl, mix ¾ cup finely diced **cooked ham** (about 3 oz.), 3 tablespoons chopped canned **green chiles,** ¼ cup chopped **green onions** (including tops), and 1½ cups (6 oz.) shredded **jack cheese.**

Ham & Swiss Cheese Tart

1 cup chopped boiled ham (about 4 oz.)
1 cup (4 oz.) shredded Swiss cheese
1 stalk celery, finely chopped

¼ cup sliced green onions (including tops)
2 tablespoons all-purpose flour
Dash *each* **of ground nutmeg and pepper**

Cottage Cheese Pastry (recipe follows)
1 egg, separated

Use your food processor to make the flaky pastry for this savory appetizer tart.

*I*n a bowl, lightly mix ham, cheese, celery, green onions, flour, nutmeg, and pepper. Set aside.

Prepare Cottage Cheese Pastry. On a floured board, roll half into an 11 or 12-inch circle; trim. Transfer to a greased baking sheet. Spread ham mixture over pastry to within 1 inch of edge; beat egg white lightly and brush over edge of pastry. Cover egg yolk and refrigerate.

Roll remaining pastry into a matching 11 or 12-inch circle; trim. Place over bottom pastry. Press edges firmly with a fork to seal. Cover and refrigerate for at least 1 hour or up to a day.

Just before baking, beat reserved egg yolk; brush over tart. Bake in a 400° oven for 20 to 25 minutes or until rich golden brown. Loosen pastry from pan and slide onto a serving board. Cut into wedges and serve hot. Makes 8 servings.

Cottage Cheese Pastry. In a food processor with a metal blade, combine 1¼ cups **all-purpose flour** and ½ cup (¼ lb.) firm **butter** or margarine, cut into pieces. Process with short bursts until blended. Add ½ cup **small curd cottage cheese** and process until dough forms a moist ball. Divide in half.

Appetizer Pizza Squares

Pictured on page 47

Pizza Dough (recipe follows)
Fresh Tomato Sauce (recipe follows)
1 jar (6 oz.) marinated artichoke hearts

3 cups (12 oz.) shredded whole-milk mozzarella cheese; or use 1½ cups (6 oz.) *each* shredded skim-milk mozzarella and jack cheeses

¼ cup grated Parmesan cheese
¼ pound thinly sliced dry salami, cut into ½-inch-wide strips

Pizza is always popular at a party. This one features a quick-rising homemade crust, fresh tomato sauce, marinated artichokes, and strips of Italian dry salami. Cut it into small squares and serve it hot from the oven.

*P*repare Pizza Dough and while it rises, prepare Fresh Tomato Sauce; set aside or cover and refrigerate for up to a day. Drain artichokes, reserving marinade; chop artichokes coarsely.

Roll each dough half into about an 8-inch circle (or roll all the dough into a 12 to 14-inch circle). Using your hands, pat and stretch dough to fit two 11 to 12-inch greased pizza pans (or one 17 to 18-inch pizza pan). Brush dough with some of the reserved marinade. Spread sauce evenly over dough and sprinkle evenly with cheeses. Distribute artichokes and salami over top.

Bake on lowest rack of a 450° oven for 15 to 20 minutes (about 25 minutes for a single large pizza) or until crust is well browned. Cut into 2-inch squares and serve immediately. Makes about 40 appetizers.

Pizza Dough. Sprinkle 1 package **quick-rising dry yeast** over 1 cup **warm water** (about 110°) in a large bowl. Let stand for 5 minutes to soften. Mix in ½ teaspoon **salt,** 1 teaspoon **honey,** and 2 teaspoons **olive oil.** Add 2 cups **bread flour;** mix to blend. With a heavy-duty mixer or wooden spoon, beat until dough is elastic and pulls away from sides of bowl (about 5 minutes). Stir in just enough additional bread flour (¼ to ½ cup) to make a soft dough.

Turn dough out onto a board or pastry cloth floured with about ¼ cup more bread flour. Knead until dough is smooth and springy and small bubbles form just under surface (5 to 10 minutes). Place in a greased bowl; turn dough to grease top. Cover and let rise in a warm place until doubled—40 to 45 minutes. (Or cover with plastic wrap and refrigerate for several hours or up to a day; remove from refrigerator and let rise for about 45 minutes before continuing.)

Punch dough down. Divide in half if using 2 pans; shape into a smooth ball.

Fresh Tomato Sauce. Heat 2 tablespoons **olive oil** in a 2-quart pan over medium heat. Add 1 small **onion,** finely chopped, and cook, stirring often, until soft. Mix in 1 clove **garlic,** minced or pressed; 5 **Italian-style tomatoes** (about ¾ lb.), peeled and finely chopped; ¼ teaspoon *each* **salt** and **oregano leaves;** ½ teaspoon **dry basil;** and ¼ cup **dry white wine.** Bring to a boil; cover, reduce heat, and simmer for 20 minutes. Uncover and cook over medium-high heat, stirring often, until sauce is thick and reduced to about 1 cup (about 15 minutes).

Camembert in Pastry

2 frozen patty shells (part of a 10-oz. package), thawed according to package directions

1 whole (7 to 8-oz.) firm Camembert or Brie cheese

1 teaspoon cumin seeds
1 egg, lightly beaten

A golden pastry jacket—easy to achieve with packaged frozen patty shells—encloses warm, cumin-sprinkled Camembert cheese.

*O*n a floured board, roll each shell into a 7½-inch circle. Place a circle on an ungreased baking sheet. Set cheese in center and sprinkle with cumin seeds. Top with remaining pastry circle. Moisten pastry edges with egg. Fold bottom edge over top and press with a fork to seal. Brush pastry with remaining egg. Slash top decoratively.

Bake in a 450° oven for about 15 minutes or until well browned. Let cool for 30 to 45 minutes to firm center before cutting into wedges. Makes 6 servings.

Savory Feta Cheesecake

Whole Wheat Press-in Pastry
1 pound feta cheese

1 large package (8 oz.) cream cheese, softened
3 eggs

Whole Greek olives or thinly sliced green onions (including tops)

Unlike sweet cheesecakes, this version teams distinctive feta cheese with mild cream cheese.

Prepare Whole Wheat Press-in Pastry.

Cut cheeses into about 1-inch chunks. Beat eggs with an electric mixer until well blended. Add cheese pieces, a few at a time, beating until smooth and well blended. Spoon into pastry. Bake in a 350° oven for 25 to 30 minutes or until center barely jiggles when gently shaken. Let cool to room temperature in pan on a wire rack. If made ahead, cover and refrigerate for up to 2 days; bring to room temperature before serving.

Remove pan sides; garnish with olives and cut into wedges. Makes 12 to 16 servings.

Whole Wheat Press-in Pastry. Combine 1 cup **whole wheat flour** and 6 tablespoons firm **butter** or margarine, cut up. With your fingers, rub mixture together until butter lumps are no longer distinguishable. With a fork, stir in 1 **egg** and mix until dough forms a ball.

Press dough in a firm, even layer over bottom and about 1¾ inches up sides of a 9-inch round spring-form pan or cake pan with removable bottom. Bake in a 350° oven for about 20 minutes or until lightly browned. Use hot or cold.

Garlic-Herb Cheesecake

Prepare **Whole Wheat Press-in Pastry** (see above). For filling, cut 3 large packages (8 oz. *each*) **cream cheese,** softened, into about 1-inch chunks. Beat 3 **eggs** with an electric mixer until well blended. Gradually add cheese, beating until smooth. Add ¼ cup **lemon juice;** 2½ teaspoons **fines herbes** (or ½ teaspoon *each* thyme, oregano, and marjoram leaves, dry basil, and summer savory); and 4 large cloves **garlic,** minced or pressed. Season to taste with **salt.** Beat until blended; then spoon into crust.

Bake in a 350° oven for 25 to 30 minutes or until center barely jiggles when gently shaken. Serve at room temperature, garnished with thinly sliced **green onions** (including tops) and cut into thin wedges. Makes 12 to 16 servings.

Crêpes Ravioli with Toasted Walnuts

12 to 14 Basic Crêpes (recipe follows)
4 cups (1 lb.) shredded fontina or Swiss cheese

6 ounces thinly sliced cooked ham, cut into julienne strips to make about 1⅓ cups
About 1 cup walnut halves

1 tablespoon butter or margarine, melted

Folded around a melted cheese and ham filling, crêpes make an easy oven-to-table appetizer.

Prepare Basic Crêpes. Mix cheese and ham. Distribute about ⅓ cup of the cheese mixture over half of each crêpe, fold over to cover filling, then fold in half again to make triangles. Place slightly apart in an 18 to 20-inch shallow baking dish or two 9 by 13-inch baking dishes. (At this point, you may cover and refrigerate for up to a day.)

Bake, uncovered, in a 450° oven for 8 to 10 minutes or just until heated through. Meanwhile, mix nuts and melted butter; sprinkle over crêpes and bake for about 3 more minutes or until nuts are lightly toasted and cheese is melted. Makes 12 to 14 appetizers.

Basic Crêpes. In a blender or food processor, whirl 3 **eggs** and ⅔ cup **all-purpose flour** (or beat with an electric mixer) until smooth; then add 1 cup **milk** and blend well. Place a 6 to 7-inch crêpe pan or other flat-bottomed pan over medium heat. When hot, add ¼ teaspoon **butter** or margarine and swirl to coat pan surface. Stir batter and pour 2 to 2½ tablespoons into pan, quickly tilting it so batter coats entire surface.

Cook until surface is dry and edge is lightly browned. Turn with a spatula and brown other side. Turn out onto a plate. Repeat, stacking crêpes as made. If made ahead, package airtight and refrigerate for up to 4 days; or freeze for up to a month. Bring to room temperature before separating. Makes 12 to 14 crêpes.

 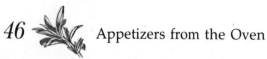

Appetizer Pizza Squares (page 45), hot
from the oven, are a snacktime success. Each serving-size
morsel stacks mouth-watering layers of fresh tomato sauce, melted cheese,
artichokes, and salami on a crisp, homemade crust.

Appetizers from the Oven

Eggplant Crêpes

2 medium-size eggplants (about 1 lb. *each*)

⅓ cup olive oil or salad oil

Marinara Sauce (recipe follows)

1 pound (2 cups) ricotta cheese

4 egg yolks

1 cup (3 oz.) grated Parmesan cheese

2 cloves garlic, minced or pressed

1 cup (4 oz.) shredded mozzarella cheese

Tender eggplant takes the place of conventional crêpes in this appealing meal opener. Long, thin eggplant slices are rolled around a ricotta cheese filling and then baked in a flavorful tomato sauce.

Slice unpeeled eggplants lengthwise about ⅜ inch thick. Discard small end slices or reserve for another use. Place slices in a single layer in two 10 by 15-inch shallow rimmed baking pans. Brush cut sides with oil. Bake, uncovered, in a 425° oven for about 20 minutes or until lightly browned.

Meanwhile, prepare Marinara Sauce.

In a medium-size bowl, beat together ricotta, egg yolks, Parmesan, and garlic. Place 2 to 3 tablespoons of the ricotta filling along side of each eggplant slice; roll up. Evenly spoon about half the sauce into a shallow 3-quart casserole. Place eggplant rolls, seam side down, in sauce. Sprinkle with mozzarella. (At this point, you may cover and refrigerate up to a day.)

Bake, uncovered, in a 350° oven for about 20 minutes (30 to 35 minutes if refrigerated) or until eggplant rolls are heated through and cheese is lightly browned. Meanwhile, reheat remaining sauce and serve to spoon over rolls. Makes about 16 appetizers.

Marinara Sauce. Heat 2 tablespoons **olive oil** in a 10-inch frying pan over medium heat. Add 1 medium-size **onion,** finely chopped, and cook, stirring often, until lightly browned (8 to 10 minutes).

Add 1 clove **garlic,** minced or pressed; 1 large can (28 oz.) **tomatoes** (break up with a spoon) and their liquid; and ¼ cup lightly packed chopped **fresh basil** or 1 tablespoon dry basil. Cook, uncovered, stirring occasionally, until sauce is reduced to about 2 cups (20 to 25 minutes). Add ½ teaspoon **sugar** and season to taste with **salt** and **pepper.** If made ahead, cover and refrigerate for up to a week; or freeze for up to 6 months. Makes about 2 cups.

Salsa Potato Skins

Pictured on page 50

5 large russet potatoes (about 3 lbs. *total*)

Chile Salsa (recipe follows)

About ⅓ cup butter or margarine, melted

¾ cup *each* shredded Cheddar and jack cheeses

For many people, the outside of a potato is the best part—especially when the crisply baked skin is gilded with two kinds of cheese, broiled, and offered as a party snack.

For extra zip, serve an easy-to-prepare chile salsa dip with the potato skins, then watch them disappear.

Scrub potatoes and pierce each with a fork. Bake in a 400° oven for about 1 hour or until potatoes feel soft when squeezed. Meanwhile, prepare Chile Salsa.

Let potatoes stand until cool enough to touch. Cut each potato lengthwise into quarters. With a spoon, scoop flesh from skins, leaving a ⅛-inch-thick shell. Reserve flesh for other uses.

Brush potato skins inside and out with butter. Place, cut side up, in a single layer on a 12 by 15-inch baking sheet. Bake in a 500° oven for about 12 minutes or until crisp. Remove from oven and distribute cheeses among hot skins, filling equally.

Broil 4 inches from heat until cheeses are melted (about 2 minutes). Serve with sauce for dipping. Makes 20 appetizers.

Chile Salsa. Stir together 1 can (8 oz.) **tomato sauce,** 1 can (4 oz.) **diced green chiles,** and ¼ cup chopped **green onions** (including tops). Pour salsa into a small serving bowl.

If made ahead, cover and refrigerate for up to a day.

Artichoke Nibbles

2 jars (6 oz. *each*) marinated
  artichoke hearts
1 small onion, finely chopped
1 clove garlic, minced or pressed
4 eggs

¼ cup fine dry bread crumbs
¼ teaspoon salt
⅛ teaspoon *each* pepper, oregano
  leaves, and liquid hot pepper
  seasoning

2 cups (8 oz.) shredded sharp
  Cheddar cheese
2 tablespoons minced parsley

To reheat these artichoke squares, bake them, uncovered, in a 325° oven for about 15 minutes.

*D*rain marinade from 1 jar of artichokes into a frying pan. Drain other jar, reserving marinade for other uses. Chop all artichokes; set aside. Heat marinade over medium heat; add onion and garlic and cook, stirring, until onion is soft.

Beat eggs. Stir in bread crumbs, salt, pepper, oregano, hot pepper seasoning, cheese, parsley, artichokes, and onion mixture. Turn into a greased 7 by 11-inch baking pan. Bake in a 325° oven for 30 minutes or until set when touched in center. Let cool slightly; cut into 1-inch squares. Serve warm, at room temperature, or cold. Makes about 6 dozen appetizers.

Crisp-baked Artichoke Appetizers

8 small artichokes
  About 1 cup fine dry bread crumbs
1 egg

¼ cup water
½ teaspoon salt
¼ teaspoon pepper

About 6 tablespoons butter
  or margarine

To eat these intriguingly shaped morsels, hold the leaves and nibble the breaded heart.

*C*ut off top half of each artichoke and trim stems to 1 inch. Snap off tough outer leaves down to pale green leaves; trim base. Slice each artichoke in half lengthwise and remove fuzzy choke. Cut each half into ¼-inch-thick lengthwise slices.

Place bread crumbs in a shallow bowl. In an-

other shallow bowl, beat together egg, water, salt, and pepper. Dip each artichoke slice in egg mixture, then in crumbs, coating both sides.

Divide butter evenly between two 10 by 15-inch rimmed baking sheets. Melt butter in a 425° oven. Remove from oven; place artichoke slices in pans and turn to coat with butter. Bake for about 15 minutes or until crumbs are brown. Serve warm. Makes about 30 appetizers.

Zucchini-Cheese Appetizer Squares

¼ cup salad oil
1 small onion, finely chopped
1 clove garlic, minced or pressed
2½ cups shredded zucchini

6 eggs, beaten
⅓ cup fine dry bread crumbs
½ teaspoon *each* salt, dry basil,
  and oregano leaves
¼ teaspoon pepper

3 cups (12 oz.) shredded Cheddar
  cheese
½ cup grated Parmesan cheese
¼ cup sesame seeds

Zucchini squares celebrate a garden's abundance.

*H*eat oil in a wide frying pan over medium-high heat. Add onion; cook, stirring, for about 5 minutes. Add garlic and zucchini; cook until zucchini is tender-crisp (about 3 minutes).

In a bowl, mix eggs, bread crumbs, salt, basil, oregano, pepper, Cheddar cheese, and zuc-

chini mixture. Spread in a greased 9 by 13-inch baking dish. Sprinkle with Parmesan and sesame seeds. Bake in a 325° oven for 30 minutes or until set when touched in center.

Let cool for at least 15 minutes; cut into 1-inch squares. Serve warm or at room temperature. Or refrigerate for up to a day and serve cold. Makes about 10 dozen appetizers.

Salsa Potato Skins (page 48), filled
with two kinds of melted cheese, are a popular party treat.
Serve them temptingly hot from the broiler with a zesty green chile salsa
for dipping, and offer with ice cold beer.

Appetizers from the Oven

Spinach Squares

2 packages (10 oz. *each*) frozen chopped spinach, thawed
3 tablespoons butter or margarine
1 medium-size onion, finely chopped

½ pound mushrooms, thinly sliced
4 eggs
1 cup half-and-half (light cream)
¼ cup fine dry bread crumbs

½ cup grated Parmesan cheese
¼ teaspoon salt
⅛ teaspoon *each* pepper, dry basil, and oregano leaves

Eat these frittata-like morsels out of hand.

Drain spinach well, squeezing out as much liquid as possible; set aside. Melt butter in a 10-inch frying pan over medium heat. Add onion and mushrooms and cook, stirring often, until onion is soft, mushrooms are lightly browned, and any liquid has evaporated (12 to 15 minutes).

In a bowl, beat eggs; stir in half-and-half, bread crumbs, ¼ cup of the cheese, salt, pepper, basil, oregano, spinach, and mushroom mixture. Turn into a well-greased 9-inch square baking pan; sprinkle with remaining ¼ cup cheese.

Bake in a 325° oven for 35 minutes or until set when lightly touched in center. Let cool slightly; then cut into 1-inch squares. Serve warm or at room temperature. Or refrigerate for up to a day and serve cold. If desired, reheat in a 325° oven for 15 minutes or until hot. Makes about 80 appetizers.

Cheese-Mushroom Fingers

½ cup (¼ lb.) butter or margarine
1 pound mushrooms, thinly sliced
1 large onion, finely chopped
2 cloves garlic, minced or pressed

1 large green pepper, seeded and chopped
10 eggs
1 pint (2 cups) small curd cottage cheese
4 cups (1 lb.) shredded jack cheese

½ cup all-purpose flour
1 teaspoon baking powder
¾ teaspoon *each* ground nutmeg, dry basil, and salt

These cheese strips will feed, and please, a crowd.

Melt butter in a large frying pan over medium-high heat. Add mushrooms, onion, and garlic and cook, stirring often, until onion and mushrooms are soft (about 10 minutes). Add green pepper and cook, stirring, for 1 more minute.

In a large bowl, beat eggs lightly. Beat in cottage cheese, jack cheese, flour, baking powder, nutmeg, basil, and salt until blended; stir in mushroom mixture. Spread in a well-greased 10 by 15-inch rimmed baking pan. Bake in a 350° oven for 35 minutes or until firm.

Let cool for 15 minutes; cut into ¾ by 2-inch strips. Serve warm or at room temperature. If made ahead, refrigerate for up to 2 days; reheat in a 350° oven for 15 minutes or until hot. Makes about 6 dozen appetizers.

Happy Hour Mushrooms

10 medium-size mushrooms (about ½ lb.)
6 tablespoons butter or margarine, softened

1 clove garlic, minced or pressed
3 tablespoons shredded jack cheese

2 tablespoons dry white or red wine
1 teaspoon soy sauce
⅓ cup fine cracker crumbs

Bubbly hot cheese-stuffed mushrooms won't last long at a party.

Remove mushroom stems; reserve for other uses. Melt 2 tablespoons of the butter; brush over mushroom caps, coating well. Stir together remaining 4 tablespoons butter, garlic, and cheese until blended. Mix in wine, soy, and cracker crumbs.

Place mushrooms, cavity side up, on a rimmed baking sheet. Evenly mound filling in each, pressing in lightly. Broil about 6 inches from heat until lightly browned (about 3 minutes). Serve warm. Makes 10 appetizers.

Substantial Snacks

Besides stimulating the appetite for a meal, appetizers can also appease that hollow feeling when it's been too long since lunch. And at parties such as those suggested on page 93, appetizers will even comprise a meal.

In any of these situations, the meat, poultry, and seafood appetizers in this chapter will fill the bill. Handsome Fig & Chicken Yakitori is a graceful introduction to a dinner featuring Asian-inspired dishes. Or offer Shrimp-filled Tomatoes as the opener of a cold summer buffet.

For many small tastes that add up to a satisfying whole, serve Glazed Sausage Balls, Sherried Oven-barbecued Spareribs, and Clams Casino.

Beef Tartare Rounds

½ pound ground beef sirloin
¼ teaspoon garlic salt
¼ teaspoon dry tarragon (optional)

⅛ teaspoon pepper
Salt
About 3 medium-size onions

1 egg
8 or 9 slices firm-textured pumpernickel bread, buttered and cut into quarters

Freshly ground meat is essential for beef tartare.

Stir together beef, garlic salt, tarragon, and pepper; season with salt. Cut onions crosswise ¼ inch thick; separate about 36 inner bite-size rings (reserve rest for other uses). Place rings side by side on a tray; press about 1 teaspoon beef mixture into each. Cover and refrigerate for at least 2 hours or up to 8 hours.

Crack egg and put yolk in a shell half (reserve white for another use); set shell in an onion ring on tray. Let guests lift an onion round onto bread and spoon on egg yolk, if desired. Makes about 3 dozen appetizers.

Carpaccio

Pictured on page 55

60 Pine Nut Breadsticks (page 38)
1¼ pounds first-cut top round, trimmed of fat, if necessary
½ cup mayonnaise

⅓ cup Dijon mustard
1 teaspoon Worcestershire
2 teaspoons lime or lemon juice

Dash of ground red pepper (cayenne)
Lime or lemon wedges

Carpaccio—thinly sliced or pounded uncooked lean beef—is an Italian appetizer innovation.

Prepare Pine Nut Breadsticks; set aside.

Wrap meat lightly and freeze just until firm but not hard (1 to 2 hours). Meanwhile, combine mayonnaise, mustard, Worcestershire, lime juice, and red pepper. Mix until smooth; refrigerate.

Up to 2 hours before serving, with a food slicer cut frozen beef across grain into paper-thin slices. (Or, using a very sharp knife, slice beef as thinly as possible; then place slices, a few at a time, between 2 pieces of plastic wrap and pound with flat side of a mallet until paper-thin.) As meat is prepared, arrange slices, separated by plastic wrap, in a large flat pan.

Cut each slice of beef in half lengthwise; then wrap a slice around each breadstick and arrange on a tray. Serve with mustard sauce and lime wedges. Makes 5 dozen appetizers.

Meat-wrapped Fruits

Pictured on page 55

1 medium-size cantaloupe
¼ pound thinly sliced prosciutto

2 pears, unpeeled
¼ cup lime or lemon juice

¼ pound thinly sliced mild cooked coppa sausage
Lime wedges (optional)

Look in an Italian delicatessen for the thinly sliced meats that complement juicy fruit wedges.

Cut cantaloupe in half lengthwise; discard seeds. Using a curved knife, cut out cantaloupe, discarding rind. Cut into about 24 long, thin wedges. Cut slices of prosciutto in half and wrap a half around each wedge. Place on a tray, cover, and refrigerate for up to 4 hours.

Cut pears in half lengthwise; discard seeds and cores. Cut into about 32 long wedges; place in a bowl. Pour lime juice over pears, turning to moisten. Cut coppa slices in half and wrap a half around each wedge. Place on a tray, cover, and refrigerate for up to 2 hours.

Arrange fruits on a serving tray. Serve with lime wedges to squeeze over cantaloupe, if desired. Makes 4 to 5 dozen appetizers.

Oven-dried Jerky

1½ to 2 pounds lean, boneless beef (flank, brisket, or round), venison, or chicken or turkey (white meat only), partially frozen

¼ cup soy sauce
1 tablespoon Worcestershire
¼ teaspoon *each* pepper and garlic powder

½ teaspoon onion powder
1 teaspoon hickory-smoke-flavored salt

Try this modern version of the traditional method of preserving meat. Here, your oven, rather than the sun, dries the thin, seasoned strips.

If the meat is partially frozen before you cut it, it's easier to slice it evenly. Cut *with* the grain of the meat if you like a chewy jerky; cut *across* the grain for a more tender, brittle product.

You can make the jerky well ahead, since it keeps indefinitely. Serve it as an appetizer with mild cheese and fresh vegetables.

*T*rim and discard all fat from meat. Cut meat into ⅛ to ¼-inch-thick slices (with or across grain—see above). If necessary, cut large slices to make strips about 1½ inches wide and as long as possible.

In a bowl, stir together soy, Worcestershire, pepper, garlic powder, onion powder, and hick-ory-smoke-flavored salt until blended. Add meat strips and mix to coat thoroughly. Let stand at room temperature for 1 hour or cover and refrigerate for up to a day.

Shaking off any excess liquid, arrange strips of meat close together, but not overlapping, directly on oven racks or on cake racks set in shallow rimmed baking pans.

Place meat in an oven set at lowest possible temperature (150° to 200°). Bake for about 5 hours for chicken and turkey, 4 to 7 hours for beef and venison, or until meat has turned brown, feels hard, and is dry to the touch. Pat off any beads of oil. Let cool to room temperature; then remove from racks and store in an airtight container.

Keep at cool room temperature or in refrigerator until ready to serve; keeps indefinitely. Makes about ½ pound.

Glazed Sausage Balls

⅓ pound bulk pork sausage
¾ pound ground pork or ground beef
½ teaspoon *each* salt, dry mustard, and crushed coriander seeds

¼ teaspoon ground allspice
1 egg, lightly beaten
¼ cup *each* fine dry bread crumbs and thinly sliced green onions (including tops)

½ cup *each* apple jelly and finely chopped Major Grey chutney
1 teaspoon lemon juice

Hot, bite-size meatballs served in an attractive chafing dish require no attention during a party. You simply provide a good supply of wooden picks in a small bowl and let guests help themselves.

You can make the well-seasoned meatballs and freeze them up to a month ahead of time. While they're browning in the oven, you prepare the chutney-based sauce that glazes them. The meatballs simmer briefly in the tart-sweet sauce; all goes into the chafing dish as the first guests arrive.

*I*n a large bowl, combine sausage, ground pork, salt, mustard, coriander seeds, allspice, egg, bread crumbs, and green onions until well blended. Shape into 1-inch balls. (At this point, you may cover and refrigerate for up to a day or freeze for up to a month.)

Place meatballs (thaw, if frozen) on rimmed baking sheets and bake, uncovered, in a 500° oven for about 8 minutes or until well browned; drain.

Meanwhile, in a wide frying pan over low heat, stir together apple jelly, chutney, and lemon juice; cook, stirring, until jelly is melted. Add meatballs; cover and simmer until glazed (8 to 10 minutes).

Transfer to a chafing dish and serve warm. Makes about 5 dozen appetizers.

Twirl Carpaccio (page 53)—thinly sliced
uncooked beef—around Pine Nut Breadsticks (page 38), then dip in a creamy mustard
sauce. Accompany with Meat-wrapped Fruits (page 53), featuring here
prosciutto with cantaloupe and coppa with pears.

Bitterballen

4 tablespoons butter or margarine
About 1½ pounds bone-in veal or pork chops *or* 1 pound ham steak
½ cup finely chopped onion
5 tablespoons flour

¼ teaspoon *each* ground nutmeg and ground white pepper
½ teaspoon salt
1 cup regular-strength chicken broth
2 eggs, separated

2 tablespoons finely chopped parsley
2 tablespoons dry sherry
About 4 cups seasoned croutons
Salad oil
Dijon mustard

With a before-dinner apéritif, the Dutch enjoy crisply coated little meat croquettes called *bitterballen*. To serve them at their best—piping hot—you can prepare them ahead, then fry just before serving. Or fry the croquettes in advance, then freeze to reheat and serve later.

*M*elt 1 tablespoon of the butter in a wide frying pan over medium heat. Add chops and cook, turning as needed, until well browned and no longer pink inside when slashed (about 5 minutes). If using ham, cook just until browned on both sides. When cool enough to handle, finely dice meat (you should have about 2 cups); set aside.

Melt remaining 3 tablespoons butter in pan; add onion and cook, stirring, just until soft. Stir in flour, nutmeg, white pepper, and salt until blended, then gradually add chicken broth; cook, stirring, until sauce boils and thickens. Remove from heat and stir in egg yolks, parsley, sherry, and diced meat; cook, stirring, just until mixture begins to bubble. Spread in a 9-inch square bak-ing dish. Cover and refrigerate until cool enough to handle (20 to 30 minutes).

In a blender or food processor, whirl enough croutons to make 2 cups fine crumbs. Shape meat mixture into 1-inch balls; roll in crumbs and place on large baking sheets. When meatballs are dry to the touch, beat egg whites just until frothy. Dip crumb-coated meatballs into egg whites, then roll again in crumbs, coating com-pletely. Cover loosely and refrigerate for at least 2 hours or up to a day.

Pour oil into a 2-quart pan to a depth of 2 inches; heat to 375° on a deep-frying ther-mometer. Cook meatballs, about 6 at a time, until golden brown (about 1 minute). Remove with a slotted spoon and drain on paper towels. Serve hot with mustard for dipping.

If made ahead, let cool completely, then package airtight and freeze for up to 2 weeks. To reheat, place frozen meatballs on rimmed baking sheets and bake, uncovered, in a 400° oven for 15 minutes or until heated through. Makes about 5 dozen appetizers.

Zesty Meatballs

1 pound lean ground beef
1 egg, lightly beaten

¼ cup *each* fine dry bread crumbs and thinly sliced green onions (including tops)
1 tablespoon soy sauce

½ teaspoon *each* salt and sugar
Horseradish Sauce (recipe follows)

A yogurt-horseradish sauce adds zest to these savory meatballs. You can make the meatballs well ahead; they'll keep in the freezer for up to a month.

*I*n a large bowl, combine ground beef, egg, bread crumbs, green onions, soy, salt, and sugar until well blended. Shape into 1-inch balls. (At this point, you may cover and refrigerate for up to a day or freeze for up to a month.)

Prepare Horseradish Sauce and set aside. Place meatballs (thaw, if frozen) on rimmed bak-ing sheets and bake, uncovered, in a 500° oven for 4 to 5 minutes or until lightly browned; re-serve meat juices. Transfer meatballs and re-served juices to a chafing dish and serve warm with sauce for dipping. Makes about 5 dozen appetizers.

Horseradish Sauce. In a small bowl, combine 2 to 4 tablespoons **prepared horseradish,** ½ cup thinly sliced **green onions** (including tops), 4 tea-spoons **dry mustard,** ¼ teaspoon **salt,** and ½ pint (1 cup) **plain yogurt** (or use 1 cup sour cream and 1 tablespoon lemon juice). Stir until well blended. Transfer to a deep bowl.

Falafel Meatballs & Mushrooms

½ cup dry falafel mix
¼ cup water
1 pound lean ground beef

½ cup finely chopped green onions (including tops)
2 tablespoons butter or margarine

36 small whole mushrooms (about 1¼ lbs.)
Tomato-based chili sauce

You'll find falafel mix in Middle Eastern markets and in some supermarkets.

*I*n a medium-size bowl, combine falafel mix and water; let stand for 10 minutes. Mix in beef and green onions. Shape into 3 dozen balls, each about 1 inch in diameter. Place meatballs in a 10 by 15-inch shallow rimmed baking pan and bake in a 450° oven for 10 to 15 minutes or until browned. Remove from oven and keep warm.

Melt butter in a 10-inch frying pan over medium heat. Add mushrooms and cook, stirring, until golden brown (about 8 minutes). To assemble, spear a mushroom and a meatball with a sturdy wooden pick. Serve with chili sauce for dipping. Makes 3 dozen appetizers.

Korean Beef Appetizers

1½ teaspoons sesame seeds
2 tablespoons sesame oil or salad oil
¼ cup soy sauce
1 clove garlic, minced or pressed

1½ teaspoons rice wine vinegar or white wine vinegar
1 teaspoon grated fresh ginger or ¼ teaspoon ground ginger
⅛ to ¼ teaspoon ground red pepper (cayenne)

1 green onion (including top), thinly sliced
1 pound boneless beef chuck, 1½ to 2 inches thick

Here's a grilled marinated beef appetizer for an outdoor party.

*I*n a small pan over medium heat, toast sesame seeds, shaking pan frequently, until golden (about 2 minutes). Whirl very briefly in a blender. Mix sesame seeds, oil, soy, garlic, vinegar, ginger, red pepper, and green onion. Cut meat across grain into very thin 3-inch-long slices. Add to marinade; mix well. Refrigerate for at least 4 hours or up to a day.

Lift out meat strips and place directly on a lightly greased, very closely spaced grill (or thread on bamboo skewers and place on grill) 4 to 6 inches above a solid bed of glowing coals. Grill, turning once, until just browned (about 1 minute per side). Transfer to a platter; provide wooden picks. Makes about 2 dozen appetizers.

Ham & Papaya Pupus

Pictured on page 7

1 large firm-ripe papaya, peeled, halved, and seeded
1 piece cooked ham (½ lb.)

Seasoned Butter Sauce (recipe follows)

The Hawaiians call their appetizers *pupus*. This simple meat and fruit combination will delight tastes anywhere.

*C*ut papaya and ham into ¾-inch cubes. To assemble, thread a papaya cube, then a ham cube, onto a wooden pick. (At this point, you may cover and refrigerate for up to a day.)

Prepare Seasoned Butter Sauce. Brush pupus with sauce and place on a lightly greased grill 4 to 6 inches above a solid bed of glowing coals. Grill, turning once, for 6 to 8 minutes. Or broil 3 to 4 inches from heat, turning and basting once, until lightly browned (6 to 8 minutes). Makes about 3 dozen appetizers.

Seasoned Butter Sauce. In a small bowl, stir together 3 tablespoons **butter** or margarine, melted; 2 tablespoons **lemon juice;** 2 teaspoons **sugar;** and ½ teaspoon **ground cinnamon.**

Mexican Chili-Cheese Logs (page 60)
pair piquantly with Crisp-fried Tortilla Pieces (page 21)
and a dash of taco sauce. Complete this appetizer fiesta with Chili Peanuts
(page 5) and refreshing Sangría (page 40).

Wine-glazed Sausage Chunks

1 pound Polish sausage (kielbasa)
1 cup dry white wine

2 tablespoons Dijon mustard
1 tablespoon Major Grey chutney

Chopped parsley

Easily made are these half-moons of spicy sausage in a mustard-wine sauce that clings to every bite.

Slice sausage 1 inch thick, then cut each slice crosswise in half. In a 12-inch frying pan, blend wine, mustard, and chutney; bring to a boil over high heat. Add sausage, reduce heat to medium-

high, and cook, uncovered, stirring occasionally, until liquid is reduced and syrupy (10 to 12 minutes).

Transfer sausage mixture to a warm bowl or chafing dish, sprinkle with parsley, and serve with wooden picks to spear hot sausage chunks. Makes 10 to 12 servings.

Italian Sausage-stuffed Mushrooms

16 medium-size mushrooms, about 2 inches in diameter
½ pound hot or mild Italian sausage, casings removed
5 green onions (including tops), thinly sliced

1 clove garlic, minced or pressed
½ teaspoon Italian herb seasoning or ⅛ teaspoon *each* dry basil, dry rosemary, and oregano and thyme leaves

1 teaspoon Worcestershire
¾ cup shredded jack cheese
About 2 tablespoons olive oil or salad oil

Piquantly hot Italian sausage together with mild jack cheese make an appetizing filling for these baked mushrooms.

Twist off mushroom stems, setting caps aside. Chop stems finely. Crumble sausage into a wide frying pan over medium heat and cook, stirring occasionally, until browned. Spoon off and discard excess fat. Add mushroom stems, green onions, garlic, herb seasoning, and Worcestershire.

Cook until all liquid has evaporated.

Remove sausage mixture from heat and stir in half the cheese. Generously brush mushroom caps with oil, then spoon about 1 rounded tablespoon of the filling into each cap. Place caps, filled side up, in a shallow rimmed baking pan. Sprinkle with remaining cheese. (At this point, you may cover and refrigerate for up to a day.) Bake, uncovered, in a 400° oven for 15 minutes or until heated through. Makes 16 appetizers.

Florentine Mushrooms

¾ pound mild Italian sausage, casings removed
1 pound spinach
1½ tablespoons chopped fresh dill or 1 teaspoon dill weed

1½ cups (6 oz.) shredded jack cheese
½ cup ricotta cheese
24 medium-size mushrooms, 1½ to 2 inches in diameter

4 tablespoons butter or margarine, melted

Stuffed mushrooms can serve as a light meal.

Crumble sausage into a wide frying pan over medium heat and cook, stirring occasionally, until well browned. With a slotted spoon, transfer sausage to a bowl. Spoon off and discard all but 1 tablespoon of the drippings; reserve in pan.

Remove and discard spinach stems; chop leaves coarsely. Add to pan, cover, and cook un-

til soft (about 1 minute). Drain spinach well, pressing out moisture. Add to sausage, then lightly mix in dill and jack and ricotta cheeses.

Twist off mushroom stems (reserve for other uses). Pour butter into a 9 by 13-inch baking dish; add mushrooms, turning to coat, then arrange cavity side up. Spoon filling evenly into each cap. Bake in a 400° oven for about 15 minutes or until hot. Makes 2 dozen appetizers.

Marrow on Toast

3 pounds beef marrow bones, cut into 3 to 4-inch lengths
2 cups water or regular-strength beef broth

2 bay leaves
1 teaspoon whole black peppers
½ teaspoon thyme leaves

2 dozen ½-inch-thick slices of thin French bread or rolls, toasted
Salt and pepper

Succulent marrow from inexpensive beef bones—some say it's the butter of beef—is a luxurious morsel to serve on toast as an appetizer.

*P*lace bones in a 3 to 4-quart pan. Add water, bay leaves, peppers, and thyme. Bring to a boil over high heat; cover, reduce heat to medium, and cook until marrow begins to shrink from sides of bones (about 15 minutes). Let stand until cool enough to handle; then shake, pull, or scoop marrow from bone and mash coarsely with a fork (reserve broth for soup).

Spread an equal amount of marrow and drippings on each slice of toast and sprinkle lightly with salt and pepper. Serve warm. For extra-crisp toast or if made ahead, arrange marrow toast in a single layer on a 12 by 15-inch baking sheet (it can stand at room temperature, lightly covered, for 4 to 5 hours). Heat, uncovered, in a 400° oven for 2 to 4 minutes or until sizzling. Makes 2 dozen appetizers.

Marrow Toast with Chives & Cheese

Prepare **Marrow on Toast** (see above), but after seasoning with salt and pepper, sprinkle evenly with 2 tablespoons chopped **fresh chives** or green onion (including top) and ½ cup freshly grated **Parmesan cheese.** Heat as directed above.

Mexican Chili-Cheese Logs

Pictured on page 58

2 eggs
2 slices firm-textured bread, torn into small pieces
1 beef bouillon cube dissolved in 1 tablespoon hot water
½ cup red taco sauce
2 tablespoons instant minced onion
1 teaspoon salt

1½ teaspoons *each* oregano leaves and chili powder
½ teaspoon ground cumin
2½ cups (10 oz.) shredded sharp Cheddar cheese
2 cloves garlic, minced or pressed
1¼ pounds bulk pork sausage
1 pound ground turkey

2 cans (4 oz. *each*) whole green chiles
1 can (4 oz.) sliced or wedged ripe olives, drained
¾ teaspoon cumin seeds
Crisp-fried Tortilla Pieces (page 21) or packaged tortilla chips
Additional red taco sauce

Pork sausage and ground turkey are rolled around a colorful filling of Cheddar cheese, green chiles, and ripe olives to make a hearty appetizer for a crowd.

*B*eat eggs in a large bowl. Add bread, bouillon mixture, ¼ cup of the taco sauce, and onion; let stand for 5 minutes. With your hands or a wooden spoon, mix in salt, oregano, chili powder, ground cumin, 1 cup of the cheese, garlic, sausage, and turkey until well blended.

Turn meat mixture out onto a 12 by 20-inch piece of foil. Pat meat into a 10 by 18-inch rectangle. Cut through meat and foil into 3 rectangles, *each* 6 by 10 inches.

Split chiles, discard seeds, and drain well on paper towels. Flatten about 2 chiles and arrange down center of each rectangle; then sprinkle with a third *each* of the olives, cumin seeds, and remaining cheese.

Starting from a long side, lift meat off foil and tightly roll each rectangle into a cylinder; firmly pinch meat together at seam and ends to seal in cheese.

Using foil to help transfer meat, place logs in a greased 10 by 15-inch rimmed baking pan; remove foil. Brush tops with remaining ¼ cup taco sauce.

Bake, uncovered, in a 350° oven for 45 minutes or until meat feels firm. Let cool, wrap in foil, and refrigerate for at least 8 hours or up to 3 days; or freeze for up to 2 months.

Prepare Crisp-fried Tortilla Pieces. Cut chilled logs (thaw, if frozen) into thin slices. Serve with tortilla pieces and additional taco sauce. Makes about 9 dozen appetizers.

Fennel-seasoned Ham & Cheese Logs

2 eggs
2 slices firm-textured bread, torn into small pieces
1 beef bouillon cube dissolved in 1 tablespoon hot water
¼ cup catsup
2 tablespoons instant minced onion

2 cloves garlic, minced or pressed
2 teaspoons dry mustard
1½ teaspoons dry basil
1 teaspoon salt
¼ teaspoon pepper
2½ cups (10 oz.) shredded Swiss cheese

1 pound *each* lean ground beef and ground turkey
½ pound sliced boiled ham
1½ teaspoons fennel seeds
Tangy Glaze (recipe follows)
Sweet pickle slices, cherry tomato halves, and cucumber slices

A variation on the previous recipe's theme, this version encloses ham and Swiss cheese in a ground beef and turkey mixture. To serve, cut the log into thin slices and offer on cocktail-size rye bread with pickles, cherry tomatoes, and sliced cucumbers to add crisp contrast.

*B*eat eggs in a large bowl. Add bread, bouillon mixture, catsup, and onion; let stand for 5 minutes. With your hands or a wooden spoon, mix in garlic, mustard, basil, salt, pepper, 1 cup of the cheese, beef, and turkey until well blended.

Shape meat mixture into 3 logs as directed for Mexican Chili-Cheese Logs (see facing page), but fill by arranging a third of the ham slices down center of each rectangle; then sprinkle

with a third *each* of the fennel seeds and remaining cheese.

Prepare Tangy Glaze. Place logs in a greased 10 by 15-inch rimmed baking pan; brush tops with glaze and bake in a 350° oven for 45 minutes or until meat feels firm. Let cool, wrap in foil, and refrigerate for at least 8 hours or up to 3 days; or freeze for up to 2 months.

Cut chilled logs (thaw, if frozen) into thin slices and arrange on a serving platter. Garnish with pickles, cherry tomatoes, and cucumber. Makes about 9 dozen appetizers.

Tangy Glaze. In a small bowl, stir together ¼ cup **catsup**, 2 tablespoons firmly packed **brown sugar**, 1 teaspoon **prepared mustard**, and ¼ teaspoon **ground nutmeg.**

Sherried Oven-barbecued Spareribs

1 side pork spareribs (3 to 4 lbs.), cut across bones into 2 strips of equal width
1 lemon, thinly sliced
1 small onion, thinly sliced

½ cup water
⅔ cup catsup
¼ cup firmly packed brown sugar
3 tablespoons sherry wine vinegar or white wine vinegar

¾ teaspoon *each* dry mustard and chili powder
¼ teaspoon *each* salt and paprika
1 tablespoon Worcestershire
⅓ cup dry sherry

Have a good supply of paper napkins handy when you serve these spareribs. They're baked in a delectable barbecue sauce accented with mustard and chili powder.

The ribs are cut Chinese style so guests can help themselves to easily manageable individual servings.

*T*rim and discard excess fat from ribs. Arrange strips in a single layer in a shallow roasting or broiler pan. Distribute lemon and onion slices evenly over meat. Pour in water. Cover with foil and bake in a 350° oven for 1 hour.

Meanwhile, in a small pan over medium heat, combine catsup, brown sugar, vinegar, mustard, chili powder, salt, paprika, Worcester-

shire, and sherry. Cook, uncovered, until sauce thickens slightly (8 to 10 minutes); set aside.

Remove ribs from oven; lift off and discard lemon and onion slices. Lift out ribs and cut between each rib bone to make small pieces. Discard pan drippings.

Return spareribs to pan in a single layer with meaty sides up; brush all over with barbecue sauce, using about half the sauce. (At this point, you may cover and refrigerate ribs and sauce for up to a day.)

Return ribs to oven and continue baking, uncovered, brushing often with remaining sauce, for 30 to 45 more minutes or until meat is well browned and fork-tender. Makes about 2 dozen appetizers.

Fried Chicken Wings with Garlic Sauce

Garlic Sauce (recipe follows)
12 chicken wings (2 to 2½ lbs. *total*)
Salad oil

2 eggs
All-purpose flour

A sweet and sour garlic-chile sauce complements the crispness of fried chicken wings, a traditional appetizer in Thailand.

*P*repare Garlic Sauce; set aside.

Cut meatiest part of chicken wing at first joint, leaving other sections together. In a deep 10 to 12-inch frying pan, heat about 1½ inches oil to 350° on a deep-frying thermometer. Pat all wing parts dry. In a shallow pan, beat eggs. Dip wings in egg, then in flour to coat lightly. Drop chicken into oil, 4 to 6 pieces at a time, and fry, turning often, until golden on all sides (about 5 minutes). Lift out and drain on paper towels. Arrange on an ovenproof tray and keep warm in a 200° oven.

For a lacy garnish, drizzle any leftover beaten egg into hot oil. Fry just until golden (about 30 seconds). Lift out with a slotted spoon and lay on wings.

If made ahead, cool, cover, and refrigerate for up to a day. To reheat, arrange wings in a single layer on a large baking sheet and bake, uncovered, in a 400° oven for 15 to 20 minutes or until heated through.

Accompany with sauce for dipping. Makes 2 dozen appetizers.

Garlic Sauce. In a 1 to 2-quart pan, stir together ½ cup **sugar,** ¼ cup **water,** ⅓ cup **distilled white vinegar,** ¼ teaspoon **salt,** and 15 cloves **garlic,** crushed. Cover and simmer until garlic is translucent (about 10 minutes). Mix 1½ teaspoons **cornstarch** with 2 teaspoons **water.** Stir into garlic mixture; cook, stirring, until mixture boils.

In a blender or food processor, combine garlic mixture, 8 more cloves **garlic,** and 1 **fresh hot chile,** 3 inches long, cut up; whirl until puréed. Use at room temperature. Makes about 1 cup.

Spinach-wrapped Chicken with Curry Mayonnaise

Pictured on page 2

2 whole chicken breasts (about 2 lbs. *total*)
1 can (14½ oz.) regular-strength chicken broth

¼ cup soy sauce
1 tablespoon Worcestershire
1 bunch spinach (about 1 lb.)

8 cups boiling water
Curry Mayonnaise (recipe follows)

Fresh spinach leaves are wrapped around seasoned chicken chunks and secured with wooden picks to make tidy appetizer packages.

Set out a bowl of zesty mayonnaise dip, accented with curry and chutney, to serve with the chicken.

*I*n a 10-inch frying pan, combine chicken breasts, chicken broth, soy, and Worcestershire. Bring to a boil over medium heat; cover, reduce heat, and simmer until chicken is fork-tender (15 to 20 minutes).

Lift chicken from broth and let cool slightly. Remove and discard skin and bones, then cut meat into 1-inch chunks.

Wash spinach. Remove and discard spinach stems, keeping leaves whole; place leaves in a colander. Pour boiling water over leaves; drain thoroughly, then set aside to cool.

To assemble, place a chunk of chicken at stem end of a spinach leaf. Roll over once, fold leaf in on both sides, and continue rolling around chicken. Secure end of leaf with a wooden pick. Refrigerate for at least 1 hour or up to a day. Meanwhile, prepare Curry Mayonnaise and serve with chicken for dipping. Makes 4 to 5 dozen appetizers.

Curry Mayonnaise. In a small bowl, combine ¼ cup *each* **mayonnaise** and **sour cream,** 2 teaspoons **curry powder,** 2 tablespoons chopped **Major Grey chutney,** and 1 teaspoon grated **orange peel;** mix until smoothly blended. Cover and refrigerate for at least 1 hour. Makes about ⅔ cup.

Tropical fruits alternate with curried
chicken chunks on bamboo skewers to make hot, broiled
Curried Chicken & Fruit Kebabs (page 64). You can use either papaya or
kumquats, along with banana and pineapple.

Curried Chicken & Fruit Kebabs

Pictured on page 63

3 whole chicken breasts (about 3 lbs. *total*), split, skinned, and boned

¾ cup bottled oil and vinegar salad dressing

2 teaspoons curry powder

2 to 3 medium-size green-tipped bananas

1 medium-size papaya or 20 to 25 preserved kumquats, drained

About 2 cups fresh pineapple chunks

⅓ cup honey

Lime wedges

Chunks of chicken breast, marinated in an oil and vinegar dressing, alternate with lively tropical fruits on small bamboo skewers for this glistening hot appetizer. The marinade, with the addition of honey, then becomes the basting sauce for the kebabs.

Most of the preparation can be done a day ahead: cut up the boned chicken and marinate it; peel the fresh pineapple and papaya, and cut into chunks. Wait until it's time to assemble the skewers to peel and slice the bananas.

Cut chicken into bite-size pieces (you should have at least 5 dozen). Mix salad dressing and curry powder in a medium-size bowl; gently stir in chicken, coating all pieces. Cover and refrigerate for at least 2 hours or up to a day.

Shortly before cooking, peel bananas and cut into 1-inch slices; brush with marinade from bowl. Peel, halve, and seed papaya; cut into 1-inch cubes. To assemble, thread chicken alternately with 1 piece *each* pineapple, banana, and papaya on bamboo skewers. Stir honey into remaining marinade and brush generously over kebabs.

Broil 3 to 4 inches from heat, basting and turning once, until chicken is lightly browned and no longer pink inside (12 to 15 minutes *total*). Serve with lime wedges. Makes about 20 appetizers.

Fig & Chicken Yakitori

Teriyaki Sauce (recipe follows)

5 large ripe figs, stems removed

4 green onions (including tops)

5 chicken thighs (about 1½ lbs. *total*), boned and skinned

Lemon wedges

The liveliest scene at many parties is the kitchen—or wherever food is being prepared. If this sounds familiar, why not feature foods that involve the guests in the tasks at hand. When you're cooking some of the appetizers on the barbecue or hibachi, let a few willing friends tend these unconventional chicken kebabs as they sizzle on the grill. They cook in minutes.

The sweet-salty flavors of a teriyaki marinade complement both the morsels of smoky chicken and the fruit and green onions that bracket them.

Prepare Teriyaki Sauce. While it cools, cut figs lengthwise into quarters and cut green onions into 1½-inch lengths; cut each thigh into 4 equal-size pieces.

Combine figs, onions, and chicken in a bowl and pour sauce over. Cover and refrigerate for about 30 minutes.

Thread 1 piece *each* chicken and fig and 3 or 4 pieces green onion near ends of 20 small bamboo or metal skewers; reserve sauce. (At this point, you may cover and refrigerate for up to 6 hours.)

Place skewers on a greased grill about 2 inches above a solid bed of glowing coals. Grill, turning once and basting occasionally with reserved sauce, until chicken is no longer pink in center when cut (3 to 4 minutes on *each* side).

Arrange on a tray and serve with lemon wedges. Makes 20 appetizers.

Teriyaki Sauce. In a 1 or 1½-quart pan, combine ½ cup **sake** or dry sherry and ¼ cup *each* **soy sauce** and **sugar**. Bring to a boil, stirring until sugar is dissolved. Let cool to room temperature. If made ahead, cover and refrigerate for up to a week.

64 Substantial Snacks

Sautéed Chicken Livers with Cucumber

1 medium-size cucumber
1 pound chicken livers
　Salt and ground white pepper
3 tablespoons butter or margarine

1 tablespoon salad oil
2 cloves garlic, minced or pressed
1 teaspoon grated fresh ginger or ¼ teaspoon ground ginger

¼ cup rice wine vinegar or white wine vinegar
　Chopped parsley

Offer livers with picks or hot buttery toast strips.

*P*eel, halve, and seed cucumber; cut each half into about ¼-inch-thick slices. Set aside.

Cut chicken livers in half; pat dry with paper towels. Sprinkle lightly on all sides with salt and white pepper. In a 12-inch frying pan over medium-high heat, melt butter with oil. Add chicken livers, about half at a time, and cook, turning often, just until well browned on all sides

(livers should still be pink inside). Remove livers as they brown and keep warm.

Remove pan from heat and add garlic, ginger, and vinegar. Return to heat and cook, stirring constantly, until pan drippings are mixed in and liquid is reduced and syrupy (1½ to 2 minutes). Add cucumber, then livers, stirring just until heated through. Turn into a warm serving dish, sprinkle with parsley, and serve with wooden picks. Makes about 20 appetizers.

Glazed Turkey-Sausage Squares

2 eggs, beaten
2 teaspoons *each* salt, dry mustard, and ground coriander
1 teaspoon ground allspice

¾ teaspoon pepper
1 large onion, finely chopped
2 cloves garlic, minced or pressed
½ cup fine dry bread crumbs

2 pounds ground turkey
¾ pound bulk pork sausage
⅓ cup *each* apple jelly, finely chopped chutney, and raisins

Jelly and chutney coat hot meat morsels.

*I*n a large bowl, mix eggs, salt, mustard, coriander, allspice, pepper, onion, and garlic; blend in bread crumbs, turkey, and sausage.

Press meat mixture into an ungreased 10 by 15-inch rimmed baking pan. Bake in a 425° oven for 12 minutes or until firm and browned at edges. Let cool on a wire rack for 10 minutes.

Holding meat, tip pan to drain off fat.

In a small pan over medium heat, melt jelly with chutney; spread over meat. Cut into 1-inch squares, top each with a raisin, and serve warm.

If made ahead, cover lightly and refrigerate for up to 2 days; or freeze for up to a month. Reheat meat squares (thaw, if frozen), uncovered, in a 400° oven for about 8 minutes or just until hot. Makes about 9 dozen appetizers.

Pickled Herring

1½ cups or 2 jars (6 to 8 oz. *each*) marinated or wine-flavored herring fillet pieces
1 carrot

1 small red onion
1 teaspoon whole allspice, slightly crushed
⅓ cup distilled white vinegar

1 cup water
⅔ cup sugar
1 bay leaf

Because it begins with prepared herring, this traditional Swedish dish goes together quickly. Offer it with sour cream.

*D*rain liquid from herring; thinly slice carrot and onion.

Alternate layers of herring, carrot, onion, and allspice in a deep, 4-cup container until all are used. In a small bowl, stir together vinegar, water, and sugar; pour over herring. Tuck in bay leaf. Cover and refrigerate for at least a day or up to 4 days. Makes about 3 cups.

Salmon cured with salt, sugar, and
dill becomes the Scandinavian delicacy, *gravlax*. Carve it
in slanting slices and offer with tart-sweet Mustard Sauce and thinly sliced bread.
The recipe for Appetizer Salmon is on page 67.

Smoked Trout Strips

1 boneless butterflied smoked trout (8 to 12 oz.)

About ¼ cup large capers, well drained

¾ cup whipping cream

1 tablespoon lemon juice

⅛ teaspoon salt

Dash of ground white pepper

2 tablespoons prepared horse-radish

Watercress sprigs or butter lettuce leaves

Lemon wedges

Accompany these tender trout bits and their zesty dip with small squares of pumpernickel.

Carefully remove and discard skin from trout. Cut each fillet in half lengthwise, then crosswise into ½-inch-wide strips. Place a caper in center of each strip, then spear with a wooden pick. If made ahead, refrigerate for up to a day.

In a small bowl, whip cream with lemon juice, salt, and white pepper until stiff. Fold in horseradish. Place bowl of creamy dip in center of a serving platter and surround with trout strips on a bed of watercress. Garnish with lemon. Makes about 4 dozen appetizers.

Salmon Tartare

1¼ pounds salmon fillet

4 teaspoons lime or lemon juice

1 tablespoon *each* chopped capers and minced shallots

2 teaspoons minced fresh marjoram or dill, *or* ¾ teaspoon dry marjoram leaves or dill weed

4 slices toast, crusts trimmed

4 pieces canned roasted red pepper or pimento, ½ by 3 inches *each*

12 whole chives

8 to 12 lime or lemon wedges

A cousin to classic beef tartare, this refreshing version is made with salmon.

If salmon is fresh, wrap and freeze until firm (about 6 hours) to kill any parasites that may exist. Thaw slightly for easier slicing. With a sharp knife, remove and discard skin and any brown flesh from salmon, peeling skin back. Chop pink flesh finely.

In a bowl, mix salmon, lime juice, capers, shallots, and marjoram. Mound on a serving platter. Cut toast diagonally in half. Garnish salmon with roasted pepper, chives, lime, and toast. Makes 2 to 2½ cups.

Appetizer Salmon

Pictured on facing page

1 salmon fillet, 12 to 15 inches long

¼ cup *each* salt and sugar

1 teaspoon dill seeds, crushed

Mustard Sauce (recipe follows)

Dill sprigs or ferns

Lemon and cucumber slices

Drained capers

Use only very fresh salmon for this cured fish appetizer from Scandinavia.

Wipe salmon dry. Cut away small bones on edges; use tweezers to pull out any bones from center. Place, skin side down, in a flat glass baking dish. Mix salt, sugar, and dill seeds; sprinkle over salmon in a thick coat. Cover dish tightly. Refrigerate, elevating end of dish with larger end of fillet about 2 inches, for about 12 hours, emptying pool of liquid in dish several times.

Prepare Mustard Sauce; set aside. Discard any remaining salt mixture from fish. Cut into thin, slanting slices, cutting each slice away from skin. Arrange on a platter with dill sprigs, lemon, cucumber, and capers. Accompany with sauce. Makes 4 to 5 dozen appetizers.

Mustard Sauce. Stir together 2 tablespoons **Dijon mustard,** 1 tablespoon **sugar,** 1½ tablespoons **white wine vinegar,** 1 teaspoon **lemon juice,** ½ teaspoon **salt,** and 1 teaspoon finely chopped **fresh dill** or ¼ teaspoon dill weed. With a fork, blend in ⅓ cup **salad oil.** Makes about ⅔ cup.

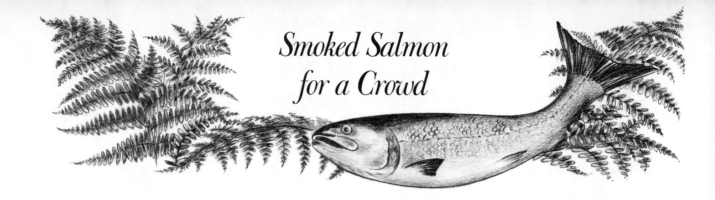

Smoked Salmon for a Crowd

Salmon, smoked at home in a covered barbecue, makes a splendid centerpiece for a party buffet. Traditional accompaniments are cream cheese and dark bread or Mini-Bagels (page 38).

Adding chips or tiny sticks of aromatic woods to the fire flavors the fish. Hickory is a favorite, but other kinds of woods you can use include alder, apple, cherry, mountain mahogany, and mesquite.

Here's the equipment you'll need to smoke fillets from a whole, large salmon: a covered barbecue, cheesecloth, hickory or other wood chips, charcoal briquets, a small barbecue or old metal pan for igniting additional coals, and an accurate oven thermometer.

Smoked Salmon

1 **whole salmon (7 lbs.), cleaned, head and tail removed, and cut lengthwise into 2 boneless fillets**
Salt Brine (recipe follows)
Syrup Baste (recipe follows)
Salad oil

Use tweezers to remove any small bones remaining in salmon fillets; arrange salmon in a shallow pan. Prepare Salt Brine and pour over fish. Cover and let stand at room temperature for 2 to 3 hours or refrigerate for up to 6 hours. Drain fish, rinse, and pat dry.

Place fillets, skin side down, on several layers of paper towels; let stand at room temperature for 30 minutes. Arrange fillets, skin side down, on a double thickness of cheesecloth; cut cheesecloth to shape of fish.

Open vents of barbecue. Mound 12 charcoal briquets in center of lower rack; ignite. Place about 1 cup hickory chips in water to cover; let stand for 20 minutes (or longer, if package directions so indicate). Meanwhile, prepare Syrup Baste.

When coals are completely covered with gray ash (30 to 40 minutes), push 6 of them to one side of barbecue, 6 to opposite side. Drain hickory chips well; sprinkle about ½ cup over each group of coals.

Brush top grill with oil and set in place. Position salmon fillets, side by side, cheesecloth side down, in center of grill (no part of fish should be directly over coals); lightly brush with some of the baste. Place oven thermometer in center of grill; cover barbecue.

Meanwhile, in another small barbecue, ignite 12 more briquets. Soak 1 more cup hickory chips in water to cover.

When salmon has cooked for 30 minutes, check thermometer (it's important to maintain a temperature of 160° to 170°). Add about 6 more hot coals to each side of barbecue (all 6 if temperature is below 160°, fewer than 6 if it's above 170°). Drain hickory chips well and sprinkle about ½ cup over each group of coals.

Use a paper towel to blot any white juices from fish so tops remain dry and shiny; lightly brush with baste. Cover and continue cooking.

Continue adding hot coals and soaked, drained hickory chips every 30 minutes or as needed to maintain temperature of 160° to 170°. Each time, blot fish and brush with baste. Cook for a total of 2½ to 3 hours or just until fish flakes when prodded in thickest part with a fork.

Carefully slide fillets onto baking sheets and let cool slightly; then cover and refrigerate until chilled or for up to 2 weeks.

To serve, carefully remove cheesecloth and place fillets on a large serving board. Cut each fillet into slanting slices, cutting each slice away from skin. Makes about 50 servings (about 5 pounds).

Salt Brine. In 2 quarts **water,** dissolve 1 cup **salt** and 1½ cups **sugar;** add 3 tablespoons **coarsely ground pepper** and 3 **bay leaves.**

Syrup Baste. Stir together ¼ cup **maple-flavored syrup,** 2 tablespoons **soy sauce,** ¼ teaspoon *each* **ground ginger** and **pepper,** and 1 clove **garlic,** minced or pressed.

Tofu Tuna Puffs

About 1 pound medium-firm tofu
1 can (about 6½ oz.) tuna, drained
1 egg
2 tablespoons finely minced green onion (including top)

1 tablespoon finely chopped fresh coriander (cilantro) or 2 teaspoons dry cilantro leaves
1 teaspoon baking powder

½ teaspoon salt
¼ teaspoon pepper
Salad oil
Soy sauce

Tofu, high-protein soybean curd cake, is sold in oriental food stores and in many supermarkets.

*I*n a colander, drain tofu for about ½ hour. Press through a fine wire strainer into a bowl or thoroughly mash with a fork. Discard any liquid. Flake tuna; add to tofu, stirring until blended.

In another bowl, beat together egg, green onion, coriander, baking powder, salt, and pepper. Add egg mixture to tofu and tuna, stirring until well blended. Shape into 1-inch balls and drain on paper towels.

In a deep frying pan, heat oil to 375° on a deep-frying thermometer. Lower tofu balls into hot oil and cook until golden brown (2 to 3 minutes). Drain on paper towels. Serve hot.

If made ahead, cool thoroughly, cover, and refrigerate for up to a day. Reheat puffs on a rimmed baking sheet in a 300° oven for 10 minutes or until heated through.

Serve with wooden picks and soy sauce for dipping. Makes about 3 dozen appetizers.

Shrimp-filled Tomatoes

Pictured on page 71

8 Italian-style tomatoes (about 1¼ lbs. *total*)
2 tablespoons mayonnaise

½ teaspoon lemon juice
1 teaspoon Dijon mustard
½ cup frozen tiny peas, thawed

6 ounces small cooked shrimp
Salt and pepper

Flavorsome Italian-style tomatoes make perfect containers for a colorful shrimp salad.

*C*ut tomatoes in half crosswise. With a small spoon, scrape out and discard seeds. Drain tomato halves, cut side down, on paper towels.

Meanwhile, in a medium-size bowl, mix mayonnaise, lemon juice, mustard, peas, and shrimp. Season to taste with salt and pepper. Fill tomato halves with shrimp mixture, using about 1 tablespoon for each. If made ahead, cover and refrigerate for up to a day. Makes 16 appetizers.

Parsley Shrimp Balls

10 ounces small cooked shrimp
4 ounces Neufchâtel cheese, softened

3 tablespoons finely chopped celery
1 clove garlic, minced or pressed
¼ teaspoon liquid hot pepper seasoning

1 teaspoon soy sauce
About ⅔ cup finely chopped parsley

Shrimp balls are tasty, low-calorie hors d'oeuvres.

*S*et aside 40 whole shrimp for garnish; coarsely chop remaining shrimp.

Beat together cheese, celery, garlic, hot pepper seasoning, and soy until very smooth. Stir in chopped shrimp just until blended. Refrigerate for about 1 hour or until firm.

Sprinkle parsley on a piece of wax paper. Shape 1 teaspoon of the cheese mixture into a ball, then roll in parsley to coat. Spear reserved shrimp on wooden picks and stick a pick into each ball. Cover and refrigerate for at least 2 hours or up to a day. Makes about 40 appetizers.

Baked Shrimp with Garlic

½ cup olive oil
1 clove garlic, minced or pressed
¼ teaspoon salt

1 pound medium-size raw shrimp (30 to 32 per lb.), shelled and deveined

1 tablespoon finely minced parsley

You marinate the shrimp up to a day ahead of time; then pop them in the oven and offer them piping hot to your guests.

Stir together oil, garlic, and salt in a shallow baking dish. Add shrimp, turn to coat with marinade, and sprinkle with parsley. Cover and refrigerate for at least 4 hours or up to a day.

Bake, uncovered, in a 375° oven for about 10 minutes or until shrimp turn pink. Serve hot, with wooden picks to spear. Makes about 30 appetizers.

Barbecued Shrimp

1 can (8 oz.) tomato sauce
½ cup molasses
1 teaspoon dry mustard
Salt and pepper to taste

Dash of liquid hot pepper seasoning
¼ cup salad oil
⅛ teaspoon thyme leaves

2 pounds medium-size raw shrimp (30 to 32 per lb.), shelled and deveined

A sweet and sour sauce flavors these appetizer shrimp. Since they cook very quickly, they're perfect when you're entertaining at an outdoor barbecue. But they can also be cooked inside—simply slip them under the broiler just until they turn pink.

In a large bowl, stir together tomato sauce, molasses, mustard, salt, pepper, hot pepper seasoning, oil, and thyme until well blended.

Add shrimp, turning to coat with marinade. Cover and refrigerate for at least 4 hours or up to a day.

Lift shrimp from marinade, thread on skewers, and place on a greased grill 6 inches above a solid bed of low-glowing coals. (Or place on a rimmed baking sheet and broil 6 inches from heat.) Cook, basting frequently and turning once, until shrimp turn pink (about 4 minutes per side). Makes about 5 dozen appetizers.

Pop-open Barbecue Clams

About 36 clams (suitable for steaming), scrubbed

½ cup (¼ lb.) butter or margarine

French bread, cut into chunks

Cooked to order over glowing coals, these succulent clams with their buttery juices invite guest participation at an outdoor gathering. Arrange the well-scrubbed clams in a bowl beside the barbecue. Alongside, provide a supply of paper napkins, forks for spearing the clams, and a basket with chunks of crusty French bread for dunking.

Place clams in a bowl adjacent to barbecue. Set grill 3 to 5 inches above a solid bed of glowing coals. Place butter in a 1½ to 2-quart pan on grill slightly away from coals so butter melts without burning.

Set each clam on grill until it begins to open (about 3 minutes); turn and continue cooking until clam pops wide open. Protecting your fingers with a napkin, hold clam over butter pan to drain clam juices into butter. To eat, spear clam with a fork and dip in butter mixture; dunk bread into butter mixture. Makes about 3 dozen appetizers.

A refreshingly light salad of tiny
shrimp with peas fills small Italian tomato halves. Serve
these enticing Shrimp-filled Tomatoes (page 69) with your favorite apéritif
or with a glass of chilled white wine.

All about Caviar

Caviar—the very word bespeaks luxury. The finest is among the world's most expensive foods. But other kinds offer good taste at all price levels.

True caviar is made from the roe (eggs) of sturgeon. The roe of other fish, such as salmon and whitefish, can also be prepared like caviar. After separation from the connective membrane, the eggs are firmed by salt or brine into sparkling beads of various colors, sizes, and textures.

For many years, costly Russian and Iranian caviar has dominated the market. As imported caviar prices have risen, the American caviar industry—once larger than Russia's—has revived.

A small amount of Pacific sturgeon caviar is available in West Coast specialty markets. Atlantic sturgeon are providing larger quantities to the East Coast. Good news for enthusiasts is the appearance of fresh whitefish caviar—sold as golden caviar—from the Great Lakes.

Types of Caviar

Caviar is sold fresh, frozen, or pasteurized (in jars). Here are some readily available kinds.

Sturgeon caviar. Imported caviars are usually identified by the variety (beluga, osetrova, sevruga) and the processing method (*malossol* means lightly salted). The roe varies in size and is gray to black. Domestic caviars may be labeled as Pacific, Atlantic, or American sturgeon.

Top-quality bulk or vacuum-packed fresh sturgeon roe, the most costly, sets the standards; it has a subtle saline flavor without tasting fishy. Its texture is soft but not limp, and the plump, round eggs tumble apart gently. Sturgeon caviar pasteurized in jars is about a third the price of fresh. Pressed sturgeon caviar, comparable in price and also pasteurized, is made of broken eggs and has a jamlike consistency.

Salmon caviar. Alaska and Pacific Northwest salmon caviar, much less costly than sturgeon

caviar, ranges in color from light orange to bright red and is available fresh in bulk or pasteurized in jars. The eggs are very large.

Whitefish caviar. This caviar, delicate but with a decided crunch, is available fresh or frozen in its natural golden color, or pasteurized in jars and dyed to simulate sturgeon or salmon caviar. Whitefish caviar from the Great Lakes, fresh or frozen, is priced comparably to salmon caviar. Pasteurized, it costs about half as much.

Lumpfish caviar. Usually imported from Iceland, this pasteurized caviar is dyed to resemble sturgeon caviar and is comparable in taste, texture, and price to pasteurized whitefish caviar.

Storing Caviar

Store fresh and vacuum-packed caviar, tightly covered, in the coldest part of the refrigerator. Bulk caviar should be used within 2 to 3 days. Fresh whitefish caviar can be stored for up to 10 days. After opening, tightly cover pasteurized caviars and refrigerate for up to 5 days.

To reduce salt and dye content, rinse dyed whitefish and lumpfish caviar in a fine wire strainer under cold running water until fairly clear (2 to 3 minutes). Then drain, cover, and refrigerate.

Serving Caviar

An ounce of caviar is a generous serving. By using it as a finishing touch, you can stretch it much further.

The classic way to serve sturgeon caviar is on thin white toast or black bread with a few drops of lemon juice. Embellishments include sour cream, chopped green onions or chives, and mashed hard-cooked eggs. Serve other caviars similarly, adding fresh dill to the topping selection. They're also good with sour cream and chives on potato skins, thick potato chips, or omelets.

Mussel & Clam Appetizer

Red Tomato Salsa (recipe follows)
Green Cilantro Salsa (recipe follows)
About 3 pounds mussels

1 cup *each* dry white wine and water
2 tablespoons lemon juice
About 36 clams (suitable for steaming), scrubbed

Sliced French bread, lightly toasted
Lime wedges
1 or 2 small hot yellow or green chiles, seeded and minced

Chilean in origin, this seafood dish combines steamed and shelled mussels and clams, served with a pair of fresh salsas.

*P*repare Red Tomato Salsa and Green Cilantro Salsa.

Sort through mussels, discarding any with open shells that do not close when covered with water. Scrub shells well with a stiff brush under running water. Pull out or cut off tough brown hairlike byssus or "beard."

In a 6 to 8-quart kettle, combine mussels, wine, water, and lemon juice. Cover and simmer over medium-high heat just until barely open (about 5 minutes). Lift out mussels, discarding any unopened shells; let cool. Add clams, about a third at a time, to kettle, cover, and simmer just until barely open (8 to 10 minutes). Lift out clams as they open; let cool.

Remove mussels and clams from shells and pile shellfish in center of a large rimmed serving plate. If desired, garnish rim of platter with mussel shells or place a few clams back in their shells in center of platter. To serve, spoon mussels and clams onto slices of bread and top with salsas, a squeeze of lime, and a sprinkling of chile, as desired. Makes 8 to 10 servings.

Red Tomato Salsa. Finely chop 1 medium-size **onion** and cover with water; add ½ teaspoon **salt** and set aside. In a bowl, combine 2 medium-size **tomatoes**, finely chopped; 2 cloves **garlic**, minced or pressed; 3 tablespoons *each* chopped **parsley** and **distilled white vinegar**; and ¼ teaspoon **oregano leaves**. Drain onions and add half to the tomato mixture (reserve rest for Green Cilantro Salsa, below). Season with **salt** and **pepper**.

Green Cilantro Salsa. In a bowl, combine reserved chopped onion (see preceding recipe) with 1 cup chopped **fresh coriander (cilantro)**; ½ cup chopped **parsley**; ½ cup **olive oil** or salad oil; 6 tablespoons **lime juice**; 3 tablespoons **distilled white vinegar**; 2 cloves **garlic**, minced or pressed; and 1 small **hot yellow chile**, seeded and chopped.

Garlic Mussels on the Half Shell

Pictured on page 74

1½ pounds mussels
1 cup dry white wine
¼ cup olive oil or salad oil

⅓ cup freshly grated Parmesan cheese
3 large cloves garlic, minced or pressed

1 tablespoon finely chopped parsley

To prepare these one-bite appetizers, broil the mussels with a topping of garlic oil and Parmesan cheese; then sprinkle with parsley. Serve with sourdough French bread.

*C*lean mussels as directed for Mussel & Clam Appetizer (above). In a large pan, combine mussels and wine. Cover and simmer over medium-high heat just until mussels begin to open (about 5 minutes). Remove pan from heat. Meanwhile, in a small bowl, stir together oil, 3 tablespoons of the cheese, and garlic; set aside.

When cool enough to handle, remove mussels from shells, discarding any unopened shells. Pull shells apart; discard half of them. Arrange remaining shells in a single layer in a shallow dish or pan that can go under broiler.

Put a mussel in each shell, then drizzle evenly with oil mixture. Broil 4 inches from heat just until cheese begins to melt and mussels are hot (about 5 minutes). Sprinkle with parsley and remaining cheese. Serve at once with wooden picks to spear mussels. Makes about 3 dozen appetizers.

Garlic Mussels on the Half Shell
(page 73), topped with olive oil, Parmesan cheese, and garlic,
are broiled until sizzling. Spear them with wooden picks and, if you like,
offer chunks of French bread to soak up the juices.

74 Substantial Snacks

Clams Casino

Rock salt
12 clams or oysters in shells

¼ cup *each* chopped green and red bell peppers

3 strips bacon, quartered
Lemon wedges

Though very easy, these clams are show stoppers.

*H*alf-fill a shallow 3-quart baking dish with rock salt. Heat dish in a 400° oven for 20 minutes. Open clams and discard top shells; leave meat and juices in bottom shells. Arrange, cavity side up, on salt, keeping shells level.

Combine peppers. Sprinkle about 1 teaspoon over each clam; top with a piece of bacon. Return to oven and bake for about 15 minutes or until bacon is crisp (do not overcook). Serve with lemon. Makes a dozen appetizers.

Scallops with Garlic

1 to 1½ pounds scallops
1 egg, beaten
¼ to ½ cup fine dry bread crumbs

5 tablespoons butter or margarine
5 large cloves garlic, minced or pressed

3 tablespoons finely chopped parsley

Crisply sautéed scallops are irresistible morsels.

*P*at scallops dry with paper towels. Dip in egg, coating well, and drain. Roll in crumbs and place slightly apart on wax paper. (At this point, you may refrigerate for up to 6 hours.)

Melt 2 tablespoons of the butter in a wide frying pan over medium-high heat. Add scallops, keeping them slightly apart, and cook until browned on one side. Add 2 more tablespoons of the butter, turn scallops carefully with a wide spatula, and cook until browned on all surfaces. Remove to a warm serving dish; keep warm.

Reduce heat to medium and melt remaining 1 tablespoon butter in pan; add garlic and parsley. Cook, stirring often, until garlic is soft and parsley is wilted. Spoon garlic mixture over scallops. Makes about 2 dozen appetizers.

Pastry Crab Puffs

About 1 cup Guacamole (page 16) or thawed frozen avocado dip
½ cup water
⅛ teaspoon salt

2 tablespoons butter or margarine
6 drops liquid hot pepper seasoning
½ cup all-purpose flour
2 eggs

1 tablespoon finely minced green onion tops or chives
½ pound crab meat
Salad oil

The same eggy, quickly cooked pastry that makes cream puffs forms the base for these puffy, deep-fried nuggets of crab.

*P*repare Guacamole; set aside.

Combine water, salt, butter, and hot pepper seasoning in a 2-quart pan. Bring to a full rolling boil over high heat; add flour all at once, remove pan from heat, and stir vigorously until mixture forms a ball and leaves sides of pan. Beat in eggs, one at a time, until mixture is smooth and shiny. Add green onions and crab; stir until blended. Let cool for about 15 minutes.

In a deep frying pan, heat 1½ to 2 inches oil to 370° on a deep-frying thermometer. Drop dough by teaspoonfuls into hot oil and fry, turning occasionally, until golden brown on all sides (about 3 minutes). With a slotted spoon, remove from oil and drain. Keep warm in a 200° oven until all are fried. Serve warm.

If made ahead, cool, cover, and refrigerate for up to a day; or wrap airtight and freeze for up to a month. Reheat puffs (thaw, if frozen) on a baking sheet in a 350° oven for 7 minutes or until hot. Offer Guacamole for dipping. Makes about 3 dozen appetizers.

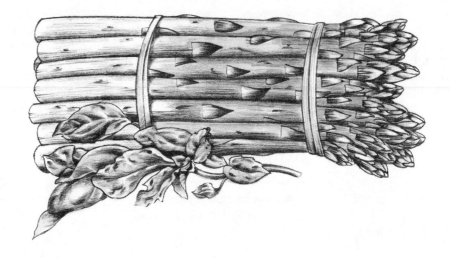

Salad, Soup & Pasta

O pening a meal with an appetizer
served as a first course adds a note of
elegance to a dinner party. Whether
it's an intimate gathering of just a few people or an ambitious undertaking for a dozen
or more, an appetizer course provides an in-
triguing prelude.

In this chapter, we present light, temptingly arranged salads and vegetables, hot
and cold soups, and some irresistible pasta
dishes. You're sure to find just the right appetizer to complement the rest of your meal.
And don't forget that many of these selec-
tions, such as Mushroom Bisque and Springtime Pasta with Shrimp, will be equally
appealing for a light lunch or late-evening
supper.

Shrimp Avocado Salad with Pistachio Nuts

Pictured on page 79

¼ cup salad oil
¼ cup white wine vinegar
¼ teaspoon salt
2 cloves garlic, minced or pressed

12 medium-large shrimp (about ¾ lb. *total*), cooked, shelled, deveined, and chilled
2 medium-size ripe avocados

2 tablespoons salted pistachio nuts, coarsely chopped
Butter lettuce leaves

A generous sprinkling of green pistachio nuts provides a crunchy contrast to the creamy avocado and tender shrimp in this first-course salad, served in avocado shells.

The nuts are usually sold in the shell, but it takes only a few minutes to prepare the quantity needed.

*I*n a small bowl, thoroughly blend oil, vinegar, salt, and garlic. Slice 4 of the shrimp lengthwise; cut remaining shrimp into ½-inch pieces. Add shrimp to oil mixture and set aside.

Halve avocados lengthwise and remove pits. With a spoon, carefully scoop out bite-size chunks of avocado and add to shrimp mixture, stirring to coat well; reserve avocado shells. If made ahead, cover avocado mixture and shells and refrigerate for up to 6 hours, gently blending mixture once or twice.

Set aside shrimp halves and fill shells with remaining avocado mixture; then top each with 2 shrimp halves. Sprinkle with pistachios. Line 4 salad plates with lettuce leaves and arrange a filled shell on each. Makes 4 servings.

Celery Root & Shellfish Salad Plate

½ cup whipping cream
1½ teaspoons lemon juice
¾ teaspoon dry tarragon or fennel seeds
½ pound scallops, cut into bite-size pieces
2 cups water
½ cup distilled white vinegar

¾ pound celery root, scrubbed and peeled
2 tablespoons salad oil
1 tablespoon finely chopped shallots or red onion
Salt
¼ pound *each* crab meat and small cooked shrimp

¼ cup finely chopped watercress or parsley
12 Belgian endive leaves or small inner romaine leaves
12 paper-thin lemon wedges
Watercress or parsley sprigs
Freshly ground pepper

Actually two salads in one, this combination can be served either as a first course or for an elegant light lunch.

Celery root's tough, knobby exterior masks a tender, creamy white interior with a celery-like flavor. You'll find it in the produce section of many markets in autumn and winter.

*I*n a 1½ to 2-quart pan, combine cream, lemon juice, and tarragon. Bring to a boil; add scallops, reduce heat, and simmer, uncovered, just until barely translucent in center (about 1½ minutes; cut to test). With a slotted spoon, transfer scallops to a bowl; cover and refrigerate until cool. Boil cream mixture over high heat until reduced to ⅓ cup (about 1½ minutes). Cover and refrigerate until cool.

Meanwhile, in a 3 to 4-quart pan, combine water and vinegar. Begin cutting celery root into matchstick pieces; as you begin, bring water mixture to a boil over high heat. Add freshly cut celery root; when mixture returns to a boil, cook, uncovered, until celery root is tender-crisp (about 30 seconds). Drain, discarding cooking liquid. In a bowl, combine celery root, oil, and shallots; season to taste with salt. Cover and refrigerate for at least 1 hour or up to a day.

In a bowl, blend cream mixture and scallops with crab and shrimp; season to taste with salt. Cover and refrigerate for at least 1 hour or up to a day. Just before serving, mix half the chopped watercress with scallop mixture and the remainder with celery root mixture.

For each serving, mound a fourth of each salad on a salad or dinner plate. Alongside, place 3 endive leaves and 3 lemon wedges. Garnish with watercress sprigs; offer pepper to sprinkle over individual servings. Makes 4 servings.

Warm Green Salad with Mussels

1½ pounds mussels
1½ cups dry white wine
1 bottle (8 oz.) clam juice

1 medium-size carrot, finely chopped
1 small onion, finely chopped
1 small head butter lettuce

4 cups finely shredded mustard greens
½ cup whipping cream

Hot mussels in wine sauce, nestled in a bed of greens, produce a dramatic first-course salad.

Sort through mussels, discarding any with open shells that do not close when covered with water. Scrub shells with a stiff brush under running water. Pull out brown hairlike byssus or "beard."

In a 5 to 6-quart pan, combine mussels and wine. Cover and boil gently over medium-high heat just until mussels begin to open (about 5 minutes). When cool enough to handle, remove mussels from shells, discarding shells and any unopened mussels. Set mussels aside.

Pour cooking liquid through a fine wire strainer into a frying pan. Add clam juice, carrot, and onion; cook over medium-high heat until reduced by half (about 15 minutes).

Meanwhile, divide lettuce equally among 4 salad plates, grouping leaves on each plate to form a cup. In center of each, mound 1 cup of the mustard greens; set aside.

Stir cream into mussel liquid. Boil, stirring often, until reduced to about 1 cup (about 15 minutes). Stir in mussels and mix gently. Spoon mussels and sauce over mustard greens. Serve immediately. Makes 4 servings.

Parisian Salad

¼ cup pine nuts
Mustard Dressing (recipe follows)

1 large ripe avocado
Tender spinach or butter lettuce leaves
1 large tomato, sliced

¼ pound pâté de foie gras, duck or chicken liver pâté, or liver sausage

Take your choice of pâté for this subtle combination of textures and flavors.

In a small frying pan over medium heat, stir pine nuts until lightly browned (3 to 4 minutes). Set aside.

Prepare Mustard Dressing; set aside. Pit, peel, and slice avocado. Line 4 salad plates with spinach; then arrange alternate slices of avocado and tomato over spinach. Cut pâté into 8 or 12 equal-size pieces and divide among plates. Spoon on dressing and sprinkle with nuts. Makes 4 servings.

Mustard Dressing. In a small bowl, thoroughly blend 2 tablespoons *each* **Dijon mustard** and **white wine vinegar;** 1 large clove **garlic,** minced or pressed; and ¼ cup **olive oil** or salad oil.

Lime-dressed Avocados

3 tablespoons *each* lime juice and salad oil

1 teaspoon sugar
⅛ teaspoon *each* crushed red pepper and oregano leaves

Salt
3 ripe avocados

Fill the hollows of avocado halves with a piquant dressing for an uncomplicated but winning salad.

In a small bowl, thoroughly blend lime juice, oil, sugar, red pepper, and oregano; season

mixture to taste with salt.

Halve avocados lengthwise and remove pits. Spoon an equal amount of the dressing into each avocado cavity, making sure all cut surfaces are coated. Makes 6 servings.

 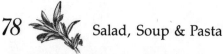

A scooped-out avocado shell holds
Shrimp Avocado Salad with Pistachio Nuts (page 77), a
handsome first course of chopped shrimp, avocado nuggets, and pistachios in a
pungent, garlic-seasoned vinaigrette dressing.

Salad with Goat Cheese Dressing

3 to 4 ounces goat cheese (such as bûcheron) or blue-veined cheese
½ pint (1 cup) whipping cream
1 teaspoon Dijon mustard

2 tablespoons *each* finely chopped shallots and parsley
Salt
1 head radicchio (about 6 oz.) *or* 2 cups finely slivered red cabbage
4 cups torn red leaf lettuce

4 cups mâche or torn butter lettuce
Freshly ground pepper

Assertively flavored salad greens—radicchio, mâche, and red leaf lettuce—are a perfect match for creamy goat cheese dressing. The greens appear seasonally in specialty markets and are also familiar to some home gardeners. If you can't obtain them, substitute red cabbage for the radicchio and butter lettuce for the mâche (also known as lamb's lettuce and corn salad).

*I*n a medium-size bowl, combine 2 ounces of the goat cheese (or all the blue cheese), cream, mustard, shallots, and parsley; with a wire whisk, blend until smooth. Season to taste with salt. Cover and refrigerate for at least 1 hour or up to a day.

Place radicchio leaves on a serving platter or line each of 8 to 10 salad plates with a leaf or two. Mix red leaf lettuce with mâche; fill radicchio leaves with mixture. (If using slivered cabbage, mix with greens.)

Spoon cheese dressing over salad. Crumble reserved goat cheese over top; offer pepper to sprinkle over individual servings. Makes 8 to 10 servings.

Cold Artichoke Mousse with Chive Cream Dressing

1 envelope plus 1 teaspoon unflavored gelatin
¾ cup water
2 packages (9 oz. *each*) frozen artichoke hearts
¼ teaspoon thyme leaves
1 whole clove garlic
⅓ cup chopped parsley

¼ cup dry vermouth
½ teaspoon *each* salt and grated lemon peel
1 tablespoon lemon juice
¼ teaspoon ground white pepper
Salad oil

½ cup whipping cream
Chive Cream Dressing (recipe follows)
Watercress sprigs or slivered butter lettuce leaves
3 tablespoons salted pistachio nuts, coarsely chopped

These molded individual salads capture the essence of artichoke flavor. Serve as a first course or with dainty sandwiches for lunch.

*I*n a small pan, combine gelatin and ½ cup of the water; let stand for 5 minutes. Place over medium heat and stir until gelatin is completely dissolved and mixture is clear; set aside.

Cook artichoke hearts with thyme and garlic according to package directions until artichokes are tender when pierced; drain well. Set aside 3 artichoke hearts, cutting each in half. Place remaining artichokes and garlic in a food processor or blender with parsley, vermouth, and remaining ¼ cup water; purée until smooth. Turn into a large bowl; mix in salt, lemon peel, lemon juice, white pepper, and gelatin mixture. Refrigerate, stirring occasionally, until mixture begins to set (30 to 45 minutes). Meanwhile, place an artichoke half in bottom of each of 6 oiled ½ to ⅔-cup molds.

Whip cream until stiff; fold into artichoke mixture. Dividing evenly, spoon into prepared molds. Refrigerate for at least 3 hours or up to a day, covering after gelatin is set.

Prepare Chive Cream Dressing. Unmold mousses onto individual salad plates and garnish with watercress. Spoon a little of the dressing over each serving and sprinkle with pistachios. Accompany with remaining dressing. Makes 6 servings.

Chive Cream Dressing. Combine ½ cup **whipping cream** with ¼ teaspoon **dry mustard,** ⅛ teaspoon **salt,** and a dash of **ground white pepper;** beat until stiff. Blend ½ cup **mayonnaise** with ¼ cup chopped **fresh chives;** fold in cream mixture. Makes about 1⅔ cups.

Dried Tomatoes—
Deliciously Different

Italian cooks have more than one way of using the small, pear-shaped tomatoes that often go into spicy sauces. Split, lightly salted, then dried, these tomatoes take on a whole new character.

The flavor of dried tomatoes is tart and intense, the texture meaty and chewy. They're as appealing a snack as any dried fruit—simply pack them loosely in a paper bag and store them at room temperature.

You'll sometimes see jars of dried tomatoes packed in olive oil with herbs. Sold in fancy food shops and delicatessens, these imported tomatoes command a fairly high price. But you can prepare dried tomatoes in oil at home, then use them in a variety of appetizers and first courses (see below).

Start with the small tomatoes sold in many markets as pear, plum, or Roma tomatoes. They're easy to recognize because of their elongated shape. Typically, they weigh 3 to 4 ounces each.

Though Italians dry their tomatoes in the sun, using your oven or a dehydrator is simpler and faster. You'll get redder tomatoes from a dehydrator, but the oven method is faster—about 7 hours compared to close to a day in a dehydrator.

Packed in olive oil, the tomatoes develop a more full-bodied taste as they age, flavoring the oil so it also becomes a delicious ingredient.

Dried Tomatoes in Oil

3 **pounds Italian-style tomatoes**
2 **teaspoons salt**
2 **sprigs rosemary** (*each* about 6 inches long) **or 1 tablespoon dry rosemary**
   About 1¼ cups olive oil

Wash tomatoes; slice lengthwise almost completely in half. Lay cut side up and sprinkle with salt.

To dry in a dehydrator, place tomatoes, cut side up, about 1 inch apart on dehydrator rack. Put in a 125° dehydrator until tomatoes shrivel to flattish, small ovals and feel dry; they should be flexible, not brittle (17 to 23 hours).

To dry in an oven, place tomatoes, cut side up, on wire racks in 2 shallow 10 by 15-inch pans. Bake in a 200° oven until tomatoes look and feel as described above (7 to 9 hours).

Pack loosely in a 1 to 1½-pint jar with rosemary. Pour in oil, covering tomatoes completely. Use immediately; or, to develop flavor, let stand, tightly covered, at room temperature for at least 3 weeks. Tomatoes keep indefinitely; use as long as oil tastes fresh. Makes about 6 ounces.

For recipes using dried tomatoes, see below.

Antipasto. Lift **dried tomatoes** from oil and arrange on a platter with sliced cold **Italian meats, small cooked shrimp, olives,** and **pickled peppers.** Moisten antipasto as desired with **seasoned tomato oil;** squeeze **lemon juice** over all.

Open-faced Sandwiches. For each, brush a side of a slice of toasted **French bread** with **seasoned tomato oil;** cover with thin slices of **fontina cheese.** Broil 6 inches from heat until cheese is melted; then top with a drained **dried tomato** and return to broiler just until warm. Sprinkle with **chopped parsley.**

Dried Tomato & Mushroom Salad. Sliver ½ cup of the drained **dried tomatoes;** mix with 4 cups torn **butter lettuce leaves** in a large bowl. In a 10 to 12-inch frying pan, combine ¼ cup of the **seasoned tomato oil** with ½ cup sliced **mushrooms.** Stir over high heat until hot; add 2 tablespoons **red wine vinegar** and season with **pepper.** Pour over lettuce and mix. Makes 4 servings.

Tomato Spread. Whirl drained **dried tomatoes** in a food processor or blender until coarsely chopped. Add **seasoned tomato oil** to moisten to spreading consistency. Spread on **toast triangles.**

Hot, mustard-flavored sauce provides the
finishing touch for first-course servings of prosciutto-
draped Hot Asparagus with Dijon Cream (page 84), a springtime treat heralding
the season of these tender emerald-green stalks.

Salad, Soup & Pasta

Pressed Leek Terrine

5 pounds small to medium-size leeks	6 cups regular-strength chicken broth	Mustard Vinaigrette (recipe follows)
1 teaspoon dry tarragon	Salad oil	

Drizzle a mustardy vinaigrette dressing over slices of this vegetable terrine, a stylish and light first-course offering.

Cut root ends off leeks and trim so only about 1 inch of dark green tops remains; reserve 10 tender green inner leaves from trimmed-off portion. Split leeks lengthwise; rinse under running water, gently separating layers to remove any soil. Rinse reserved leaves.

In a 4 to 5-quart pan, bring tarragon and broth to a boil; add leeks and reserved leaves. Cover, reduce heat, and simmer until tender (about 15 minutes). Drain (reserve broth for other uses). Separate leeks into leaves and layer flat in a well-oiled 5 by 9-inch loaf pan so dark green tops are equally distributed throughout

terrine (cut long pieces to fit pan length and patch layers to use all leaves). Oil bottom of an identical pan and set on top of leeks; put about 4 pounds canned goods or dried beans in top pan to weight leeks. Refrigerate for at least 8 hours or up to 2 days. Pour off any liquid that accumulates.

Prepare Mustard Vinaigrette. Remove weighted pan. With a sharp knife, gently cut loaf crosswise into 10 slices. Using 2 spatulas, lift out slices and arrange on a platter or individual salad plates. Spoon dressing over. Makes 10 servings.

Mustard Vinaigrette. In a small bowl, thoroughly blend ½ cup **olive oil** or salad oil, 3 tablespoons **lemon juice**, 1 tablespoon **Dijon mustard,** and ¼ teaspoon **pepper.** Season to taste with **salt.**

Potato Pancakes with Sautéed Apples & Goat Cheese

1 pound russet potatoes	Salt and pepper	¼ pound goat cheese (such as Montrachet or bûcheron), cut into 6 rounds or wedges
½ cup thinly sliced green onions (including tops)	½ to ¾ cup (¼ to ⅜ lb.) butter or margarine	
¼ cup all-purpose flour	1 large red apple	2 tablespoons finely chopped chives or green onion tops
2 eggs	½ cup large walnut pieces (optional)	
2 tablespoons milk or water		

Sparkling cider goes well with these embellished potato pancakes. You can make the pancakes ahead; crisp them just before serving.

Peel and finely shred potatoes (to prevent discoloration, immerse in cold water as cut). In a large bowl, thoroughly beat together the ½ cup green onions, flour, eggs, and milk. Lift out potatoes, squeezing out excess water; stir into egg mixture. Season to taste with salt and pepper.

In a 10 to 12-inch frying pan over medium heat, melt 2 tablespoons of the butter. For each pancake, spoon 1½ tablespoons of the potato mixture into pan and spread into a 4-inch-long oval. Cook pancakes, 3 or 4 at a time, turning once, until golden (3 to 4 minutes per side); add more butter as needed. As pancakes are cooked, remove with a spatula and arrange in a single layer in 2 shallow rimmed 10 by 15-inch baking

pans. (At this point, you may cover and let stand for up to 6 hours.)

Core apple; cut into 16 to 18 wedges. In pan over medium heat, melt 2 more tablespoons butter. Add apples and cook, turning once, until slightly translucent (about 2 minutes per side). Transfer with a spatula to a shallow dish; set aside. Add walnuts, if desired, to pan and stir until lightly toasted (about 3 minutes); set aside. (At this point, you may cover apples and walnuts and let stand for up to 6 hours.)

Bake pancakes, uncovered, in a 400° oven for about 6 minutes or until crisp. Move pancakes into one pan, making 6 stacks of 3 or 4 slightly overlapping pancakes each. Arrange equal portions of apple, cheese, and walnuts, if desired, on each stack. Bake for 2 minutes or until fruit and cheese are warm. Transfer each stack to a plate; sprinkle with chives. Makes 6 servings.

Fresh Herb Timbales

2½ tablespoons butter or margarine, softened

¼ cup finely chopped shallots or green onions (white parts only)

3 eggs

½ pint (1 cup) whipping cream

⅛ teaspoon *each* ground white pepper and ground nutmeg

Minced fresh herb (amount follows for each type)

Salt

Sprigs of fresh herb to match flavor of timbales (optional)

Aromatically seasoned with your choice of basil, dill, or tarragon, these savory timbales, or custards, can open a meal or be part of a light supper. Accompaniments for the latter are suggested for each herb.

Present the timbales hot from the oven or, if you prefer, prepare them ahead and serve them at room temperature.

Thoroughly coat bottom and sides of four ½-cup timbale molds or custard cups with ½ tablespoon of the butter. Set molds in a 9 by 13-inch baking pan.

Melt remaining 2 tablespoons butter in an 8 to 10-inch frying pan over medium heat. Add shallots; cook, stirring, just until shallots begin to brown. Let cool to room temperature.

In a large bowl, beat together eggs, cream, white pepper, nutmeg, fresh herb, and cooked shallots until thoroughly blended. Season to taste with salt. Pour equal amounts of the custard mixture into molds. Place baking pan with molds on middle rack of a 350° oven and pour scalding water into pan until it comes halfway up sides of molds. Lightly cover pan with foil. Bake for 30 to 35 minutes or until custards appear set when lightly shaken. Lift molds from water; let stand until surface butter is reabsorbed (10 to 15 minutes).

Slip a knife around sides of molds and invert custards onto serving plates. Serve hot or at room temperature. Garnish with herb sprigs, if desired. Makes 4 servings.

Basil Timbales. Use 2½ tablespoons minced **fresh basil.** Serve with thinly sliced roast chicken or turkey.

Dill Timbales. Use 2½ tablespoons minced **fresh dill.** Serve with thin slices of smoked salmon or lox, poached or baked fresh salmon, or poached or sautéed small trout.

Tarragon Timbales. Use 2 tablespoons minced **fresh tarragon.** Serve with thinly sliced roast beef, lamb, or chicken.

Hot Asparagus with Dijon Cream

Pictured on page 82

20 large asparagus spears (1¼ to 1½ lbs. *total*)

½ cup dry white wine

¼ cup whipping cream

2 teaspoons Dijon mustard

4 tablespoons butter or margarine

4 thin slices prosciutto, Westphalian ham, or mild cooked coppa sausage

Freshly ground pepper

Slender asparagus spears draped with thinly sliced prosciutto and bathed in a creamy mustard sauce are a showy hot first course that's easily accomplished.

You can serve the asparagus on individual salad plates or arrange the spears on a long, rectangular serving tray.

Snap off and discard tough ends of asparagus. Peel stalks with a vegetable peeler; set aside.

In an 8 to 10-inch frying pan, combine wine, cream, and mustard. Bring to a boil over high heat, stirring constantly, and boil until mixture forms large, shiny bubbles and is reduced by half. Add butter and stir constantly until completely blended. Keep warm over lowest heat.

Place asparagus in 1 inch of boiling water in a 10 to 12-inch frying pan; boil, uncovered, just until spears turn bright green and are tender-crisp when pierced in thickest part (2 to 3 minutes). Drain well.

Arrange 5 asparagus spears on each of 4 salad plates or make 4 groups on a serving tray. Drape a slice of prosciutto over each group. Offer pepper to sprinkle and sauce to spoon over individual servings. Makes 4 servings.

 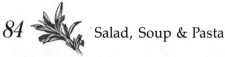

Chilled Avocado Soup

1 tablespoon salad oil
1 clove garlic, minced or pressed
½ cup chopped onion
2 large ripe avocados
¼ cup lemon juice

3 tablespoons dry sherry (optional)
1 tablespoon chicken stock base dissolved in 2½ cups hot water
¾ teaspoon liquid hot pepper seasoning

2 tablespoons chopped fresh coriander (cilantro) or parsley
2 to 2¼ cups milk
Salt
About 1 cup corn chips, coarsely crushed

Cool soup is a pleasing starter in warm weather.

Heat oil in a small pan over medium heat. Add garlic and onion; cook, stirring often, until soft (3 to 5 minutes). Let cool. Pit, peel, and slice avocados into a food processor or blender; add lemon juice, onion mixture, and sherry, if de-sired. Whirl until puréed. Add chicken broth and hot pepper seasoning; whirl to blend. Pour into a large bowl. Stir in coriander and enough milk to thin soup to desired consistency. Season with salt. Refrigerate until cold (up to 3 hours).

Before serving, stir well. Sprinkle chips over individual servings. Makes 6 servings.

Chilled Tomato-Cucumber Soup

2 tablespoons salad oil
1 medium-size onion, chopped
1 medium-size carrot, shredded
2 teaspoons dry basil
¾ teaspoon sugar
⅛ teaspoon ground white pepper

1 can (1 lb.) tomatoes
1 can (14½ oz.) regular-strength chicken broth
1 large cucumber, peeled and coarsely shredded

¼ cup thinly sliced green onions (including tops)
1 teaspoon Worcestershire
Salt
½ cup whipping cream
1 tablespoon lemon juice

Reserve a few cucumber or green onion slices to garnish each serving of this creamy soup.

Heat oil in a 2-quart pan over medium heat. Add onion and carrot; cook, stirring often, until onion is soft (8 to 10 minutes). Stir in basil, sugar, and white pepper. Add tomatoes (break up with a spoon) and their liquid. Bring to a boil; cover, reduce heat, and simmer for 20 minutes.

In a blender or food processor, whirl tomato mixture, half at a time, until smooth. Pour into a large bowl; blend in broth, cucumber, green onions, and Worcestershire. Season with salt. Refrigerate for at least 8 hours or up to a day.

Before serving, pour soup through a fine wire strainer; discard vegetable solids. Blend in cream and lemon juice, and serve cold. Makes 4 to 6 servings.

Dutch Shrimp Soup

½ cup all-purpose flour
3 cups regular-strength chicken broth
3 cups milk

1 teaspoon *each* paprika and dill weed
¼ cup tomato paste
¼ cup finely chopped parsley
1 pound small cooked shrimp

¼ cup whipping cream
3 tablespoons lemon juice
Pepper

This quick-cooking soup is enriched with cream.

Put flour in a 5 to 6-quart pan; slowly blend in broth. Stir in milk, paprika, dill, tomato paste, and parsley. Bring to a boil over high heat, stir-ring constantly; reduce heat and simmer, un-covered, stirring occasionally, for 10 minutes. Add shrimp and cream; cook just until hot (2 to 3 minutes). Stir in lemon juice and season to taste with pepper. Makes 8 servings.

Smooth & Creamy Carrot Soup

1 pound carrots (5 or 6 medium-size)

2 tablespoons butter or margarine

1 large onion, finely chopped

2 tablespoons *each* tomato paste and long-grain rice

4 cups regular-strength chicken broth

½ cup whipping cream

Salt and pepper

Carrot curls or parsley sprigs

Carrot curls decorate this first-course soup.

Chop carrots finely (you should have about 3 cups). Melt butter in a 3 to 4-quart pan over medium heat. Add onion and cook, stirring often, until soft (6 to 8 minutes). Add carrots, tomato paste, rice, and broth. Bring to a boil; cover, reduce heat, and simmer until carrots are very tender (about 20 minutes). In a blender or food processor, whirl broth mixture, about half at a time, until puréed. (At this point, you may cover and refrigerate for up to 2 days.)

To serve, return soup to pan; add cream and bring to a simmer over medium heat, stirring occasionally. Season with salt and pepper. Garnish with carrot curls. Makes 6 to 8 servings.

Shiitake Spinach Soup

Pictured on facing page

8 to 12 medium-size fresh or 1 ounce dried shiitake mushrooms

2 tablespoons butter or margarine

1 small onion, finely chopped

3 cans (14½ oz. *each*) regular-strength beef broth

1 medium-size thin-skinned potato, peeled and cut into ½-inch cubes

1½ cups firmly packed spinach leaves (about ½ lb.)

Enoki mushrooms (optional)

Flavorful shiitake mushrooms—fresh or dried—give substance to this light beef broth.

If using dried mushrooms, cover generously with water and let stand for 30 minutes; then drain. For fresh or dried mushrooms, cut off and discard stems, and cut caps into ⅛-inch-wide slivers.

Melt butter in a 4 to 5-quart pan over medium heat. Add onion; cook, stirring often, until soft (about 5 minutes). Add broth and shiitake mushrooms. Cover and bring to a boil over high heat; add potato, reduce heat, and simmer until fork-tender (about 10 minutes).

Add spinach and cook, uncovered, until spinach is just wilted (1 to 2 minutes). Ladle into bowls and garnish with enoki mushrooms, if desired. Makes 4 to 6 servings.

Mushroom Bisque

4 tablespoons butter or margarine

1 pound mushrooms, coarsely chopped

2 large onions, sliced

2 cloves garlic, minced or pressed

⅓ cup chopped parsley

1 teaspoon thyme leaves

⅛ teaspoon ground white pepper

7 beef bouillon cubes

⅓ cup all-purpose flour

6 cups milk

Salt

Condiments: Grated Parmesan cheese, thinly sliced raw mushrooms, thinly sliced green onions (including tops), croutons, and ground nutmeg or whole nutmeg with a grater

You can make this creamy soup ahead; reheat it, uncovered, over medium-low heat, stirring often.

Melt butter in a 5 to 6-quart pan over medium heat. Add mushrooms, onions, garlic, parsley, thyme, pepper, and bouillon cubes. Cook, stirring often, until vegetables are soft. Add flour.

In a blender or food processor, whirl mushroom mixture, half at a time, with just enough milk to purée smoothly. Return to pan; add remaining milk. Cook over medium heat, stirring, until thickened. Season with salt. Serve with condiments to sprinkle over individual servings. Makes 8 first-course or 6 main-dish servings.

86 Salad, Soup & Pasta

Appealingly light Shiitake Spinach Soup
(page 86) begins with either fresh or dried shiitake mushrooms. Look for delicate, long-stemmed fresh enoki mushrooms to gracefully
complete this hot, first-course offering.

Cream of Artichoke Soup

Seasoned Artichokes (recipe
follows)

4 tablespoons butter or margarine

2 tablespoons chopped shallots

1 teaspoon dry basil

1 can (14½ oz.) regular-strength
chicken broth

½ cup whipping cream

Dry sherry

Fresh artichokes, cooked to perfection with herb seasonings, make a distinctive, creamy first-course soup.

To serve artichokes on their own as an appetizer, prepare them as for Seasoned Artichokes (see recipe below). After they're cooked, let them cool to room temperature. Then arrange them on individual salad plates and pass around a bowl of Curry Dip (page 14). Let guests use the tender bases of the leaves and the heart to scoop up the spicy sauce.

*P*repare Seasoned Artichokes; let cool. Scrape pulp from leaves, reserving pulp and discarding leaves. Scoop out and discard fuzzy center from hearts and trim fibrous exterior of stem. Coarsely chop hearts. (You should have about 3 cups *total* pulp, stems, and hearts.)

Melt butter in a 2 to 3-quart pan over medium heat. Add shallots, basil, and artichokes.

Cook, stirring often, until heated through (about 3 minutes).

In a blender or food processor, whirl artichoke mixture until puréed; then return to pan. Add broth and cream; bring to a boil. Just before serving, add sherry to taste. Makes 4 servings.

Seasoned Artichokes. Immerse 4 large **artichokes,** each about 5 inches in diameter, in water; shake to dislodge foreign matter. Snap off and discard small outer leaves. Cut off lower part of stems, leaving about 1½ inches.

In a 6 to 8-quart kettle, combine 4 quarts **water,** 2 tablespoons *each* **olive oil** and **white wine vinegar,** 1 **bay leaf,** 2 teaspoons **dry basil,** and ½ teaspoon **ground allspice.** Add artichokes. Cover and bring to a boil over high heat; reduce heat and boil gently until bases are tender when pierced (about 40 minutes). Lift out artichokes and drain well.

Lentil Cream Soup

½ cup lentils

4 cups regular-strength beef broth

1 medium-size carrot, cut into
1-inch pieces

8 to 10 parsley sprigs

¼ teaspoon whole cloves

1 tablespoon olive oil or salad oil

½ cup finely chopped shallots or
red onion

1 cup dry sherry

2 tablespoons lemon juice

1 pint (2 cups) whipping cream

½ teaspoon pepper

Edible flowers, such as pansies,
Johnny-jump-ups, or rose petals,
washed

Chive spears or finely chopped
parsley

Lentils may be hearty, traditional food, but they make a very elegant and up-to-date soup to serve as an appetizer.

In this version, whole cloves, chopped shallots, and dry sherry flavor the lentils. Cream, added just before you're ready to serve, enriches the soup.

As an extra touch, float some edible flowers in the soup tureen. They'll add color, as well as a bit of drama.

*R*inse lentils; sort through and discard any foreign matter. Drain well.

Bring broth to a boil in a 3-quart pan over

medium-high heat; add lentils, carrot, parsley sprigs, and cloves. Cover, reduce heat, and boil gently until lentils are tender to bite (30 to 40 minutes). Discard carrot, parsley, and cloves; set lentils and cooking liquid aside.

Heat oil in a 4 to 5-quart pan over medium heat. Add shallots and cook, stirring occasionally, until soft. Add sherry and lemon juice; boil over high heat, uncovered, until reduced to about ¼ cup.

Stir in lentils and cooking liquid, cream, and pepper. Bring just to a simmer, then pour into a warm soup tureen. Garnish with flowers and chive spears. Makes 6 to 8 servings.

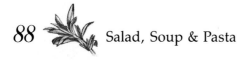

Colorful Noodles Made with Fresh Herbs

When making fresh pasta, adding a vegetable purée such as spinach to the dough gives the noodles more color than flavor. But a generous quantity of a fresh green herb not only colors the pasta, but also gives it a distinct, yet delicate, flavor and fragrance.

Choose basil, oregano, marjoram, or chives for these homemade noodles. Because of their savory flavor, they're most appealing presented simply—with a bit of butter, then a sprinkling of freshly grated Parmesan cheese, some chopped tomato, slivers of prosciutto, or lightly browned crumbled Italian sausage.

You can prepare and knead the dough by hand or with a food processor, then shape by hand or with a pasta machine (don't use an extrusion-type machine). For very tender noodles, roll the dough as thin as possible; roll it slightly thicker if you prefer noodles with a more pronounced herb flavor.

Fresh Herb Noodles

1 cup firmly packed fresh basil leaves, oregano or marjoram sprigs (woody stems removed), or coarsely chopped chives or garlic chives
1 egg
1 tablespoon water
2 to 2½ cups all-purpose flour
2½ quarts boiling salted water
    About 4 tablespoons butter or margarine, melted
    Salt and pepper

In a blender or food processor, whirl herb with egg and the 1 tablespoon water until puréed.

To mix and knead by hand, put 1 cup of the flour in a large bowl; pour in herb purée and stir with a fork until blended (mixture will be dry and crumbly). Press into a ball and turn out onto a lightly floured board. Knead, adding more flour if dough is sticky, until very smooth and elastic (10 to 15 minutes).

To mix and knead in a food processor, place 1 cup of the flour and herb purée in processor fitted with a metal blade. Process until dough forms a smooth, elastic ball (2 to 3 minutes). If dough feels sticky, add about 1 more tablespoon flour and process to blend. Cover with a bowl or plastic wrap and let rest for 30 minutes.

To roll noodles by hand, divide dough in half. On a floured board, roll one portion at a time (covering remaining portion) as thinly as possible (⅟₁₆ inch or less). Turn dough over occasionally, gradually adding about 1 cup flour to prevent sticking. If dough shrinks back as you roll, cover with plastic wrap, let rest a few minutes, then continue. With a sharp knife or noodle cutter, cut into ¼-inch (or narrower) strips.

Separate noodles and lay out on wax paper on a flat surface. Sprinkle lightly with flour. Cover while rolling and cutting remaining dough.

To make noodles with a pasta machine, cut dough into 4 equal portions. Feed one portion (covering remaining portions) through smooth rollers set on widest setting. Fold strip into thirds and feed through again. Continue until dough feels like smooth, supple leather (about 25 times), gradually adding about ⅓ cup more flour.

Set roller one notch closer and, without folding, feed dough through machine. Repeat, setting roller up one notch each time, until dough is no more than ⅟₁₆ inch thick. Feed dough through cutting blades. Arrange cut noodles as described above; then roll and cut remaining dough.

(At this point, you may roll noodles loosely in wax paper and enclose in a plastic bag; refrigerate for up to 2 days. Or wrap well and freeze for up to a month.)

To cook, drop noodles, a few at a time, into boiling salted water; stir. Cook, uncovered, until *al dente* (1 to 2 minutes for thin noodles, 3 to 4 minutes for thicker ones). Drain, shaking out excess water. On a warm platter, mix hot noodles lightly with butter, lifting gently with 2 forks. Season with salt and pepper. Makes 6 first-course servings or 3 or 4 main-dish servings.

A tangle of lemon zest flavors hearty
Scallops & Red Pepper Pasta (page 91), an inviting
starter for dinner—or equally satisfying for a light supper with just a
green salad and a loaf of French bread.

90 Salad, Soup & Pasta

Springtime Pasta with Shrimp

¾ pound asparagus
¼ pound Chinese pea pods
8 ounces medium egg noodles or 12 ounces fresh pasta, such as fettuccine
4 to 6 quarts boiling salted water

4 tablespoons butter or margarine
½ cup sliced green onions (including tops)
1 clove garlic, minced or pressed
½ pint (1 cup) whipping cream
½ cup dry white wine

⅛ teaspoon *each* ground nutmeg and ground white pepper
⅓ cup grated Parmesan cheese
½ pound small cooked shrimp
Additional grated Parmesan cheese

For an elegant pasta dish, combine emerald green, crisply cooked asparagus and Chinese pea pods (sometimes called snow peas) with tiny pink shrimp and creamy noodles.

Snap off and discard tough ends of asparagus; cut into bite-size pieces (you should have about 2 cups). Remove and discard ends and strings from pea pods. In a 3 to 4-quart pan, cook asparagus in boiling water, uncovered, for 3 minutes; add peas and cook until barely tender-crisp (about 1 more minute). Drain vegetables and set aside.

Cook noodles in boiling salted water until *al dente* (2 to 3 minutes for fresh pasta, 5 to 6 minutes for dry pasta). Drain (separately from vegetables) and set aside.

Meanwhile, melt butter in a 12-inch frying pan over medium heat. Add green onions and garlic; cook, stirring occasionally, until onions are soft and bright green (1 to 2 minutes). Add cream, wine, nutmeg, and white pepper; bring to a boil over high heat and boil, stirring occasionally, until reduced by about half (about 5 minutes).

Mix in the ⅓ cup cheese, shrimp, and vegetables just until heated through. Remove from heat; using 2 forks, stir in pasta until lightly coated with sauce. Serve immediately; offer additional cheese to sprinkle over individual servings. Makes 6 first-course servings or 3 or 4 main-dish servings.

Scallops & Red Pepper Pasta

Pictured on facing page

1 lemon
12 ounces linguine
4 quarts boiling salted water
4 tablespoons butter or margarine
¼ cup olive oil

3 large red bell peppers, seeded and cut into thin slivers
2 cloves garlic, minced or pressed
¼ to ½ teaspoon crushed red pepper
¾ cup regular-strength chicken broth

¼ cup lemon juice
1 pound scallops, cut into ¼-inch slices
¾ cup finely chopped parsley
Salt and pepper

Vibrant red pepper strips and creamy scallops team up with linguine—a perfect way to stretch a pound of seafood to make 6 first-course offerings or 3 or 4 entrée servings.

With a zester, cut peel from lemon in fine shreds (or thinly pare yellow layer of skin and cut into fine slivers); set aside, reserving lemon to squeeze for juice. Cook linguine in boiling salted water until *al dente* (about 9 minutes). Drain, rinse with cold water, and drain again. Set aside.

Melt butter with oil in a 10 to 12-inch frying pan over medium-high heat. Add bell peppers, garlic, and crushed red pepper; cook, stirring, for 1 minute. Lift out bell peppers with a slotted spoon; set aside. Add broth and lemon juice; bring to a boil. Add scallops, cover, and cook until scallops are opaque (about 3 minutes); remove from heat. Lift out scallops with a slotted spoon and add to peppers.

Add linguine to pan; heat, lifting with 2 forks, until pasta is hot. Transfer pasta and sauce to a warm serving dish; top with parsley, scallops, peppers, and lemon zest. Mix lightly and season to taste with salt and pepper. Serve immediately. Makes 6 first-course servings or 3 or 4 main-dish servings.

Gorgonzola Fettuccine

½ cup pine nuts
6 ounces Gorgonzola cheese

1½ cups whipping cream
4 tablespoons butter or margarine
1 pound spinach fettuccine

4 to 6 quarts boiling salted water
⅓ cup grated Parmesan cheese

Gorgonzola melts into a creamy sauce for pasta.

*I*n a small frying pan over medium heat, stir nuts until browned (3 to 4 minutes); cool.

Crumble Gorgonzola and set aside ⅓ cup. In an 8 to 10-inch frying pan over low heat, combine remaining Gorgonzola, cream, and butter. Heat, stirring with a wire whisk, until smooth; keep warm.

Cook fettuccine in boiling salted water until *al dente* (2 to 3 minutes for fresh pasta, 5 to 6 minutes for dry pasta). Drain and transfer to a warm rimmed platter. Pour sauce over pasta and sprinkle with Parmesan cheese. Lifting pasta with 2 forks, mix lightly with sauce. Sprinkle with pine nuts and remaining Gorgonzola. Serve immediately. Makes 6 to 8 first-course servings or 4 main-dish servings.

Angel Hair Pasta with Chèvre

6 ounces goat cheese (such as bûcheron or Montrachet), cut into chunks
1½ cups whipping cream

2 cloves garlic, minced or pressed
4 tablespoons butter or margarine
8 ounces thin pasta strands (such as capellini or vermicelli)
3 to 4 quarts boiling salted water

¼ pound sliced cooked ham, cut into thin slivers
2 tablespoons chopped parsley
¼ cup walnut halves

Thin pasta strands contrast delicately with a robust sauce of goat cheese, cream, and ham.

*I*n a 2-quart pan, combine goat cheese, cream, garlic, and butter. Stir over low heat until smooth.

Cook pasta in boiling salted water until *al*

dente (2 to 3 minutes for fresh pasta, 4 to 5 minutes for dry). Drain and transfer to a warm platter. Pour sauce over pasta; add slivered ham and parsley. Lifting pasta with 2 forks, mix lightly with sauce. Sprinkle with walnuts. Makes 4 first-course servings or 2 main-dish servings.

Camembert-stuffed Pasta Shells

Marinara Sauce (page 48) or 1 jar (15 oz.) meatless spaghetti sauce
2 tablespoons butter or margarine
1 small onion, finely chopped
2 cloves garlic, minced or pressed

8 ounces Camembert cheese, diced
1 egg
½ cup ricotta cheese or small curd cottage cheese
1 cup chopped parsley

½ cup grated Parmesan cheese
25 to 30 large seashell-shaped pasta shells
3 to 4 quarts boiling salted water

Giant pasta shells make a lusty first course or, with salad and garlic bread, a satisfying meal.

*P*repare Marinara Sauce; set aside.

Melt butter in an 8 to 10-inch frying pan over medium heat. Add onion and garlic and cook, stirring often, until onion is soft (2 to 3 minutes). Reduce heat to low, add Camembert, and stir until soft; remove from heat. In a medium-size bowl, mix egg, ricotta cheese, parsley, and ¼ cup of the Parmesan cheese; stir into Camembert mixture.

Cook pasta shells in boiling salted water un-

til *al dente* (about 9 minutes). Drain, rinse with cold water, and drain again. Stuff each shell with about 1 tablespoon of the cheese filling. Spread half the Marinara Sauce in a 7 by 11-inch baking dish or shallow 2½-quart casserole. Arrange shells, filling side up, in sauce. Spoon remaining sauce in a band over top of each. (At this point, you may cover and refrigerate for up to a day.)

Bake, covered, in a 350° oven for about 30 minutes (35 to 40 minutes if refrigerated) or until bubbly and heated through. Garnish shells with remaining ¼ cup Parmesan cheese. Makes 8 first-course servings or 4 main-dish servings.

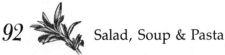

Appetizer Menus for All Occasions

Creative menus that require little last-minute preparation, yet are in perfect harmony with that special occasion, make an appetizer party easy for the hosts to manage—and for the guests to enjoy. The appetizer selection presented in each menu can provide enough food for an entire meal.

Autumn Football Buffet

This appetizer array is a versatile one—you can serve it on a tailgate before or after a game, or spread it out at halftime in front of the television set. The sausage is the only hot dish; away from home you can reheat it in a chafing dish over an alcohol or canned heat flame.

Italian Eggplant Relish (page 13) with Parmesan Pocket Bread Appetizers (page 33)

Nut-studded Garlic-Herb Cheese (page 24) with Assorted Crackers

Fennel-seasoned Ham & Cheese Logs (page 61) with Cocktail Rye Bread, Sweet Pickles, Cherry Tomatoes, Sliced Cucumber

Wine-glazed Sausage Chunks (page 59)

Spinach Squares (page 51)

Beer, Jug Red Wine, and Soft Drinks

Pre-Theater Appetizer Supper

An evening at the theater starts off festively when you share the time before the show with friends. These light offerings are just enough to carry everyone through the performance.

Sautéed Camembert (page 25) with Sliced Toasted French Bread

Shrimp-filled Tomatoes (page 69)

Ham & Swiss Cheese Tart (page 44)

Crisp-baked Artichoke Appetizers (page 49)

Apéritifs (page 40)

Holiday Hors d'Oeuvre Party

Greeting friends at an open house is a time-honored way of celebrating the holiday season. Along with an array of inviting nibbles, offer a selection of beverages, including champagne.

If you serve sweets toward the end of the afternoon or evening, look for bite-size chocolate truffles or individual pastries.

Candied Pecans (page 5)

Marinated Baby Carrots (page 6)

Cherry Tomatoes with Smoked Oysters (page 8)

Parsley Shrimp Balls (page 69)

Black Caviar Pie (page 25) with Unsalted Crackers

Glazed Chicken Liver Pâté (page 28) with Thinly Sliced Toasted French Bread

Appetizer Mini-Quiches (page 44)

Florentine Mushrooms (page 59)

Tiny Sweets (optional)

Champagne

Spring Reception

Many are the spring occasions when a light, pretty assortment of appetizers is called for— Mother's Day, weddings, anniversaries, graduation. All the appetizers below can be made ahead and refrigerated or frozen until they're needed.

Aspic-glazed Cheese (page 27) with Mild-flavored Crackers

Chèvre & Green Grapes (page 8)

Glazed Shrimp Crisps (page 11)

Beef with Pea Pods and Horseradish Dip (page 11)

Cocktail Cream Puffs with Gingered Chicken Salad (page 35)

Cheese Twists (page 37)

Fruit Punch or Sparkling Wine

Index

Portable appetizers for the patio or picnic
table include hot Onion Cheese Puffs (page 36),
and a cold assortment of Creamy Braunschweiger
Appetizer (page 19), Spinach Dip (page 14),
and crackers and vegetables for dipping.

Metric Conversion Table

To change	To	Multiply by
ounces (oz.)	grams (g)	28
pounds (lbs.)	kilograms (kg)	0.45
teaspoons	milliliters (ml)	5
tablespoons	milliliters (ml)	15
fluid ounces (fl. oz.)	milliliters (ml)	30
cups	liters (l)	0.24
pints (pt.)	liters (l)	0.47
quarts (qt.)	liters (l)	0.95
gallons (gal.)	liters (l)	3.8
Fahrenheit temperature (°F)	Celsius temperature (°C)	5/9 after subtracting 32